## Going to Blazes

alcolm Castle is the longest-serving officer on the tch in Shrewsbury, Shropshire, having spent more an thirty years at the station.

# GOING TO BLAZES

Further Tales of a Country Fireman

## MALCOLM CASTLE

An Orion Paperback

First published in Great Britain in 2015 by Orion Books
An imprint of the Orion Publishing Group Ltd
Orion House, 5 Upper St Martin's Lane,
London, WC2H 9EA

An Hachette UK Company

© Malcolm Castle 2015

A CIP catalogue record for this book
is available from the British Library.

ISBN   978 1 4091 50985

Typeset by Input Data Services Ltd, Bridgwater, Somerset

Printed and bound by CPI Group (UK) Ltd, Croydon, CR0 4YY

The Or[...]on Publishing Group's policy is to use papers that are [natu]ral,
renew[...] and recyclable products and made from wood grow[n] in
sustainab[...] processes are [res]pected
to conf[...] country of [ori]gin.

# 1

# The Happiest Horse in All Shropshire

'Open the blinkin' windows, someone! I'm going to pass out from the smell of Dodger's size-twelve feet in a minute!'

I smiled broadly as I heard Ben's shout. He was behind me, on the back seat of the fire engine. We were about to roll around the first of the many wide curves and sharp corners in the centre of my beautiful Shrewsbury.

We'd been playing our usual sweaty, psychotic game of volleyball in the station yard when the fire call had come through. Now we were sweating and still mildly psychotic in the fire engine. It was only ten-thirty in the morning but the summer sun was already surprisingly strong. For some reason the cab's windows had all been closed while it stood idle in the appliance room. Jumping in had been like climbing into a greenhouse. Riding in it was like sitting in a sauna with all our clothes on. And I swear you really could pass out from the smell of Dodger's feet.

'Put your blinkin' boots on, Dodger, or the rest of us will have to get into our chemical protection suits,' Ben was moaning as we passed the railway station and turned right on to Smithfield Road.

'Well if you'd just get your elbow out of my face and stop

hogging all the space back here, I'll have enough room to move,' Dodger replied.

I smiled again from the safety of the driver's seat. Pulling your kit on in a moving vehicle isn't easy at the best of times. But the three men we had on the back seat today – Dodger, Ben and new recruit Nicholas – were easily the biggest on the watch. Ben was six foot four like me, Nicholas was at least six foot two, and Dodger, although short, was easily as wide as the other two. All three had shoulders as broad as small cars. No wonder they were making a lot of noise.

'If you don't stop mithering I'll get Windsor to stop off at Oswestry and replace the lot of you with one of the retained crews. Happen they'll be twice as good as you and give me half as much trouble,' declared Joe from the passenger seat alongside me. Joe was the equally tall Sub-Officer or Sub-O on Red Watch. He was the number two on the team and the most senior fireman in the vehicle. He had the world's most bushy eyebrows – surely a fire hazard in themselves – and one of the world's sternest faces. He was a tough taskmaster too. He had high standards and expected everything to be done by the book. Today, though, as we picked up speed and fresh air finally began to swirl through the cab, he was smiling. He waved to a group of kids standing goggle-eyed at the roadside as we passed Telephone House. He gave a salute to a couple of pretty mums standing with their pushchairs alongside the river. And he sat back in his seat and gave a contented sigh as we crossed the Welsh Bridge and headed out west towards the border with Wales.

'I might have a bit of shut-eye. Wake me up if you get lost,' he joked as I steered the vehicle on to the Welshpool Road, heading to the western edge of our patch. In the back of the cab the sudden silence suggested that the others had got kitted up at last and were ready to settle down for the long ride to the job. We were relaxed and happy that day because we weren't on an emergency call to fight a fire or face yet another tragic car accident. No, that warm and sunny day at the end of July we were heading deep into the countryside to rescue a pony. Or, to be strictly accurate, our new colleague Nicholas was on his way to rescue a pony.

That crucial detail had been decided the moment the call came in. The pony in question wasn't in mortal danger. But it was in a bad place. The farmer said it had done what ponies often do: jumped over a gate or pushed through a gap in a hedge. It had trotted off on a little adventure. And it had got itself in trouble.

'It's ended up slap bang in the middle of a slurry pit,' we'd been told. 'It's up to his neck in it. They can't get it out. And it's as whiffy as hell.'

All eyes had turned to Nicholas.

'You're joking,' he'd begun weakly.

'I've never been more serious in my life. This one's for you, jockey. Enjoy it,' Joe had told him as we'd made our way into the appliance room. I'd all but laughed out loud. Four years ago, when I'd been the new recruit or 'jockey' on Red Watch, all these mucky, dodgy jobs had come to me. The jockey is always the one who has to get his hands dirty, lose his dignity and end up the laughing stock of the county. How great to think that I'd handed over the mantle at last.

'We didn't cover this kind of thing in training,' Nicholas had muttered to me as we swung ourselves up on to the fire engine.

I smiled again. At twenty, Nicholas was nearer my age than anyone on Red Watch. We'd got on well from the start. He'd been working in a timber yard before signing up, so he was exactly the kind of practical man we needed. He had short light hair and he was almost always smiling. He was a keen fisherman and a big drinker. 'A good lad, plenty of potential, but he's got a bit of an overactive sense of enthusiasm,' was the only negative comment the old-timers could think of to say about him. I had a horrible feeling they'd said the same about me, back in the day. They probably still did, if I was honest.

I swung the fire engine round the next in a long line of sharp bends and took a deep breath of fresh, country air. The hedgerows were getting higher and if the fields weren't quite golden they were certainly a healthy shade of bronze. I gazed ahead when we topped the crest of a small hill. Welshpool was probably somewhere in the far distance. Long before it were a host of homesteads and hamlets. The roads were narrowing sharply and the countryside threw up more sharp corners than a corkscrew. I thanked my lucky stars that I was behind the wheel and not stuck on the back seat like the others. I got crippled with travel sickness sometimes – a fact that the other lads found completely hilarious in a fireman. Far too many times, heading back from a shout, the driver would swing outrageously wide around a bend just to see how green my face would turn.

Out on this part of our patch the bends were particularly intense. Many of them hit as you plunged down into a hidden hollow, one of Shropshire's dark, tree-covered dips where water crashed over the stones in a barely mapped network of brooks and streams. I looked over to Joe as I pulled us out of one such dip. His eyes were still shut. I glanced at the folded-up map on his lap. We might be needing that soon. This was part of the county where the lanes had no names. Whole clusters of farms and houses seemed to manage just fine without any names either. Some of the villagers we came across swore blind they were from one place, when the map said something entirely different.

'I read somewhere that there used to be a Royal Mint in these parts. Back in the tenth century,' Dodger said, waking up and interrupting my thoughts as we gained a bit of gradient.

'You've never read anything but car magazines in your life. And you still struggle with the long words in those,' Ben hit back.

'I read more than you think, old man. And I read about gold coins being made in this part of Shropshire.'

'You know what? I think you might be right about there being an old mint in Shrewsbury itself. Don't know where, though,' said Nicholas, keen to join in the conversation the way the jockey always was.

'It's not in the town,' said Dodger. 'It was put out in the country to protect it. They reckoned it needed to be well hidden. It could be out here.'

'Actually, Welsh gold is supposed to be really valuable. If we find some of that, we're quids in,' said Ben, perking up all of a sudden.

'So you're saying we do a bit of treasure hunting while we're out here on a shout?' I asked with a smile.

'Well, it couldn't do any harm. It would get you that BMW you're always dreaming about.'

'A straight six, 323i. In midnight blue,' I said dreamily.

'Before anyone tries to find buried treasure I suggest we find the farm we're looking for and get the owner's horse back in its field,' said Joe, lifting those terrifying eyebrows and gazing out over the countryside ahead. 'And I suggest we look pretty sharpish because I reckon we're somewhere close.'

'It's up ahead. Four hundred yards, then we take a right and we're within spitting distance,' I said, with far more confidence than I felt.

'I think you're wrong, Windsor,' came Ben's voice from behind. 'We should have gone left at that last junction, not right. We've been to this farm before. We had a barn fire there back in '78.'

'We have never been here before. Not in '78, not ever,' said Dodger.

'So where was that fire?'

'It was in your dreams, mate. We've never been anywhere near here. And we shouldn't be here now. We've gone wrong. You need to turn us round, Wins.'

'Have we got a better map? Isn't that one old?' I asked, flashing a glance to the one Joe was now unfolding on the passenger seat. One of the other benefits of driving is that you can push all the map-reading questions on to others. Occasionally we'd joke about some *Star Trek* or *Blake's 7*-type future when moving maps would spring up on electronic screens in front of us and disembodied computer voices would guide us directly to our destination. Until that far-off day I had to rely on Joe poring over a particularly tatty map to my left and a host of testosterone-fuelled opinions floating across from the cab behind me.

'If I see anyone, I'll ask them. Someone has to know where Nottage Farm is,' I declared after a while.

You could feel the disgust that comment generated. It swamped the whole cab and seeped into every corner. If disgust had a smell, then our cab reeked that day. 'Ask someone? *Ask someone?* I don't think so, matey!' Dodger declared to general agreement.

And so we continued our rambling and extended tour of the glorious highways and byways of western Shropshire.

'With a bit of luck the horse will have got itself out and washed itself down by the time we arrive,' said Nicholas hopefully at one point.

'You should be so lucky, jockey, you should be so lucky,' said Joe. And at that moment we saw the sign. It was old, crooked and made of rotten wood. But it was there. Nottage Farm. We opened a gate, thundered over a couple of vast cattle grids, twisted round some high-camber corners and parked in a surprisingly tidy yard.

'Time to get your hands dirty,' the others were telling Nicholas as we all climbed out of the cab. 'Let's hope you brought a clothes peg to put on your nose.'

However, Nicholas soon began to cheer up as we approached the farmhouse door. We all did, truth be told. The farmer who came out to greet us was a rough-and-ready-looking man about my dad's age. He was wild and weather-beaten, as country farmers always were. He was also flat-nosed, big-eared, had next to no chin and a funny little squint, so at first it was hard to tell who he was talking to. He was wearing tatty old tweed trousers and a stained brown corduroy shirt that looked older than me. His hair appeared to have been cut by someone wearing a blindfold – while on a rollercoaster ride. Completing the picture were teeth so yellow they were almost orange. But none of this was what snagged our attention and improved Nicholas's mood no end.

'This is my daughter, Melody,' the man growled as another figure joined him on the doorstep. 'It's her pony that's got itself in trouble and caused all the fuss.'

'Hello, Melody,' five grown men said in embarrassing unison.

Could this vision of loveliness really be his daughter? Could someone that old and messy be the parent of someone this young and beautiful? Because Melody was the best-looking girl we'd seen in quite some time. She was probably in her early twenties. She obviously helped out on the farm, because she looked as weather-beaten as her dad. But Melody was weather-beaten in a blonde, Californian, sun-kissed, Olivia Newton-John kind of way. She was wearing faded blue jeans and an ordinary checked shirt. But she was wearing them in a very Daisy Duke kind of way. She was smiling nervously, revealing perfect white teeth, perfect pale blue eyes, perfect soft skin. I could have gone on – and the other lads would do just that for weeks and weeks afterwards.

And of all people it was Nicholas who was going to impress the soft white cotton socks off her.

'I'm the one who'll be saving your pony, Melody,' he said firmly, leaping in to stake out his turf in case Joe changed his mind and gave the task to someone else. 'It will be dangerous and things could get messy,' he continued shamelessly, as if he was about to storm the *Death Star* or raise the *Titanic*. 'Things could go badly wrong,' he added, showing a previously hidden talent for melodrama. 'There will be no easy choices in how we do this. But we will do it. *I* will do it, Melody. I will rescue your pony.'

I flashed a look at Joe. His mouth was wide open. Was he outraged or impressed by the youngster's sheer front? I think it was the latter. I think there was the start of a twinkle in his eye as he stepped back a little. I felt myself do the same. Nicholas wanted to take charge. He wanted to run the show. Could he do it? I think we all knew it was going to be a hell of a lot of fun finding out.

The farmer gave us some background before the main event. 'We've tried everything to get it out of the pit ourselves. We've tried goading it and we've tried slapping it. We've tried to scare it with the sound of the tractor and we've tried getting a rope round its neck and pulling it free. But we don't want to injure the horse. You've got the kit we need. We wouldn't have called you if we hadn't had to.'

Nobody doubted that closing statement. Farmers were proud in our part of the world. Maybe they are everywhere. They work hard and they don't like wasting anyone's time. They're also the most resourceful and tight-fisted people on earth. If they can do a job themselves, they'll do it. Even if they have to improvise with utterly inappropriate tools. If there was any way this man could have got his daughter's pony free on his own, he'd have done it long ago.

Nicholas thrust out his chest as he joined us getting the various ropes, strops and slings out of their compartments and preparing for battle. For all the comedy value and the schoolboy sniggering, we were still a pretty professional team. Joe took the lead, explaining what we'd have to do. There were no real surprises, for in truth it wasn't the world's most complicated operation. This was one of those jobs you did all the time in the country Fire Service. Animals were forever getting lost or trapped. We were always lassoing them or looping them up in ropes and slings and pulling them back to freedom. We did it in rain, snow and hail. Doing it on a glorious early summer's day was chicken feed. Which perhaps explained why the twinkle was back in Joe's eye.

'Now, young Nicholas, when I tasked you with this job I was perhaps being a little hasty,' he began. 'If you should like to step aside, one of your more experienced colleagues would be happy to take your place.'

'I wouldn't hear of it,' Nicholas said, his chest puffed out even further, his eyes firmly aimed at the lovely Melody.

So we approached the slurry pit where the rescue would be carried out.

'My horse's name is Bradforth,' said Melody. Five men turned and nodded at her as if she'd been reciting the most beautiful poetry. Bradforth was a fine but filthy beast; more horse than pony, in my far from expert view.

'And three years old,' called Melody. Four more words of pure poetry.

We stood and surveyed the scene. Slurry pits come in all shapes and sizes; this one was twenty feet by ten and about five feet deep. They're all filled with . . . well, let's just say that grass might smell quite fragrant when it goes in the mouth of a cow, but once it comes out the other end it has a very different and extremely unpleasant odour. After a run of hot summer days the thick crust that forms on top of the slurry resembles solid earth. This is why they're always fenced off. Unfortunately, the fence around this one was made up of two loose strands of rusty barbed wire fixed to a few ancient and rotten wooden posts.

The odoriferous contents of the pit were swirling and splashing about as this most spirited of ponies kicked about and drew air in and out of its hefty flanks. And the whole place stank. It was truly rank. Clouds of black flies buzzed around angrily. Much as we all wanted to impress Melody, the sight of great drools of saliva falling from Bradforth's mouth had us all taking a step back. Suddenly no one was keen to take Nicholas's place in getting the animal rescue slings around the huge and glistening body of this very agitated, very angry animal.

Joe got us started: 'Let's get a fore-end loader over here.'

When that was done, the next step was to get a lifting chain attached to the fork of the fore-end loader and position it above the animal, ready to secure the slings that would hoist Bradforth out of the pit and on to firm ground.

Once the loader was in position we were ready for the main event. It was now up to Nicholas to wade into the waste to thread the two slings underneath Bradforth's belly.

And this was where things began to go horribly wrong.

We talked tactics one last time as the farmer, whose name we didn't know, and Melody, whose name we would never forget, looked on. Melody then stepped forward. We held our breaths. 'It's so smelly in there. It's such a horrible thing for you to do. I'm so very, very grateful,' she said poetically.

'It's my job,' Nicholas said ridiculously.

A few moments later, things took a dramatic turn. The four of us were stationed at various points around the pony and the slurry pit – edging back as far away from the latter as we possibly could. Nicholas, meanwhile, was right in the thick of things, chest-deep in the slurry, reaching in up to his shoulder to drag the slings from one side of the horse to the other. Bradforth, sweat glistening on his back and running down in to the contents of the pit, was finally still. And then Nicholas was too. He quite literally froze.

I was the closest to him at that point, and I could sense that something bad had happened. I swear he had gone pale. All the flirting and the jokes were over. I had no idea what was going on, but it seemed to be serious.

'Oh my God,' Nicholas said. His voice was unusually quiet. That made his words all the more memorable.

'What is it?' Melody and her dad asked, almost in unison.

'What's up, jockey?' said Joe, moving round from the far side of the slurry pit much faster than his size and age might have suggested he was capable of.

Nicholas looked from face to face. He really was white as a sheet. 'I think there's something wrong,' he said.

'What do you mean?'

'I'm checking.' Nicholas moved his arm around. He moved his arm forward then back. He reached a little further under the pony's stomach. Then he looked up.

'He's badly injured. The poor bugger's split his stomach open. He must have caught it on the barbed wire. You need to get a vet here quick. I think he's going to die. I can feel his spleen hanging out.'

Everyone went deathly quiet and things began to move fast. The farmer set off towards the farmhouse to get to the phone. His daughter, younger and faster, ran past him.

'Is it bad?' Joe asked, when they were out of earshot.

'It's bad. I think it's very bad,' Nicholas said.

Joe nodded, grim-faced. All the fun was forgotten now. I looked up at the barbed-wire fences all around us. Barbed wire is essential in the countryside, but it's a curse as well. Over the years we've attended countless horrible scenes where animals have got caught up in it. We've seen the damage it can do. We've seen the pain in so many animals' eyes and we've seen a fair few of them die. That day we could only hope the vet would get there fast enough.

'You want to climb out?' Joe asked as Nicholas wrinkled up his nose against the smell. Flies were landing on his hair and his ears. He shook his head violently as one took aim at his left eyelid.

'I don't think I can. If I do, I reckon he'll die. I'm trying to push his insides back in. I'm trying to hold him together. If I move now, it's all over.'

Joe nodded as the farmer finally came out of the house and headed back towards us. 'Vet is on his way now,' he said authoritatively as we considered our next move. Melody was at his side. A tall, willowy woman who had to be Melody's mum was there too, and a teenage boy.

'He knows the way? He'll be here fast?' Nicholas asked from the pit.

'Fifteen minutes. Maybe less.'

'Then let's work this out,' said Joe, calling us all together. 'Can we move the horse?' he asked Nicholas.

'I don't know. The wound has to be pretty deep. I reckon I've got its spleen in my hand. If we move the animal, it will fall right out. Being in all this crap might be what's saved him. It's kept things together, at least for a while.'

Joe nodded. 'In that case, I say we stay as we are. As soon as the vet's here, we'll lift the horse out. Then he can do what he has to do.'

'I'll get a hose ready. The vet will need him to be clean. We'll need water,' said Dodger, and the rest of us headed over to the appliance to get the pump in gear and the on-board tank opened so we could supply it. Nicholas had stayed where he was, up to his shoulders in the gently steaming and horribly smelly slurry pit. His hand was trying to hold together the animal's innards. His face was looking older, paler.

I caught his eye at one point as the others busied themselves. He shook his head ever so slightly. It was obviously bad. I glanced at the pony itself. How long had it been in pain? Did it know we were here to help? I looked away. It's crazy to put human feelings into animals' minds. It's stupid to think you know how they're feeling. I thought I'd read something in those dark, impassive and injured eyes, but I shook my head. Better to focus on helping the others and getting this job done.

Fortunately the vet was as good as the farmer's word. We heard his Land Rover just under fifteen minutes later. A cloud of summer dust blew up above the hedgerows in its wake. He was a jolly, surprisingly rotund man in his early forties, with a hefty black bag in his right hand. He seemed capable, listening carefully to what we told him while surveying the scene. Then he told us to get the horse out so he could do whatever needed to be done.

'We'll do it slowly but smoothly,' Joe said when we were ready for the off. He nodded at the farmer to get the tractor started. Nicholas, still at the horse's side, still keeping the wound together, stopped things for a moment. 'Melody, are you sure you want to see this? It won't be very nice,' he warned.

'I want to see it. It's my horse. I'm not going anywhere.'

The vet gave us the nod. He had all manner of sterilising and stitching kit out and standing by. The tractor engine roared and the loader was raised, lifting Bradforth slowly from the slurry. Nicholas held on to the spleen with both hands. As the horse was lifted, we washed all the brown smelly slurry off its body until the injury was clear of the pit. Bradforth tried to struggle against the movement of the lifting slings, but with a tractor providing the power, the slings were going to carry on raising him regardless.

I wondered how bad it would be as the pony stepped out on to the dry, muddy earth around the pit. His four long, sinewy legs buckled but straightened fast. Was horse blood red? It was a stupid question, but for some reason I couldn't remember. Would it be brown, or black, if it had been out of his body for some time? Would it be visible amid all the slurry? And wouldn't the wound be horribly infected by now? And made worse by all the flies and whatever else was swimming around in there?

Thoughts raced through my mind as Dodger directed water over the animal's back and down over his flanks. There, I thought, would be the torn skin and the terrible flesh wound. The ruptured spleen that would be half in and half out of the horse's body. Except, it wasn't. As the steaming slurry was washed away, the horse appeared to be entirely intact. We could see no injury on it at all.

The horse shook itself. It stood tall. It kicked its legs. It threw back its head. It tossed its mane. It was in rude health. It actually looked proud, happy, strong and in near tip-top condition. So what the hell was going on?

It was clear everyone was asking themselves the same question. Melody, her dad, their family, the vet and us. Oh, and Nicholas most of all.

'I swear – I swear he was all cut up and injured,' he began. 'There was a wound, a big, deep flesh wound. This horse was in a terrible state. I could feel it. Its spleen was outside of its body. I had it in my hand.'

And in that moment he, and the rest of us, got it.

This very happy horse was actually a stallion. As he shook himself again and gave a loud whinny of pure contentment, we knew, suddenly, why he had stood so still and stayed so silent in the pit. Bradforth hadn't been in agony. He hadn't been injured. He'd been having the time of his life with that nice new fireman reaching down at his side and—

'Oh my God. Oh my God. I didn't, did I?' Nicholas asked, appalled, as he realised what he'd done. 'So all that time I was holding on to his—?' He stopped, unable to complete the sentence.

'Yes, you were, sonny. All that time. And the wee pony didn't even have to buy you dinner first!' Dodger said as Melody let out a whoop of laughter and clasped her hand to her mouth.

\*

The long ride back in the fire engine wasn't a lot of fun for Nicholas. Despite an ice-cold hose down and a bit of carbolic from the farmer's outhouse, he still stank to high heaven. In truth, the trip wasn't a great deal of fun for us either.

'I think I preferred the smell of Dodger's killer feet,' Ben said early on. But then our conversation moved on. It was time to do what firemen do best. It was time to take the mickey out of the new boy.

'Remember that other horse we pulled out of the old mine-shaft on the Stiperstones?' Dodger pitched up as Nicholas's new ordeal began.

'We'll get Nicholas to help out if that sort of thing comes up again. He'll be able to pull it off all on his own,' Ben threw in.

Back at the station the story travelled fast. It probably got exaggerated out of all proportion too. And so a day or two later the love letters and the fake phone messages started to come in.

*Dear Nicholas, you never ring, you never write*, the first of the notes began, written in a childish hand and signed: *A Very Happy Horse.*

*Phone message received for Nicholas Beardsmore. From someone called Bradforth. Says: When are you coming back to the farm?* read the next, taped to the outside of his locker for the start of our night shift.

*To the nice young fireman from Shrewsbury – I'm feeling frisky, let's make hay together. Your ever-loving (it) pony, Bradforth*, read yet another.

To his credit, Nicholas was up for it. He laughed like the rest of us. He was due to get married the following spring, but he told plenty of jokes about the horse trotting into the church, all dressed in white, when the vicar gets to the part about speaking now or forever holding your peace.

16

All the same, there was a hint of worry on his face sometimes as the jokes continued.

'How long will this last?' he asked me in the bar at the start of an evening shift a week or so later. 'Will they ever forget it?'

'Of course they will,' I told him. 'In about twenty years.'

He sat and gazed out from the open window of the mess room. In the distance, across the yard and over the nearby trees, the setting sun was turning thin layers of cloud into a collage of rich pinks and orange. Then they all turned to gold as the midsummer sun made its final fall from view. A gang of what I think were starlings started to fight, noisily. Nicholas sighed.

'It's never going to be forgotten,' he said ruefully as the rest of the gang stormed into the room, making enough noise to scatter every starling within about a mile.

'Yes it will. As soon as someone else makes an equally stupid mistake on another shout,' I told him.

Nicholas looked glumly across at me. 'But what if that's me as well?' he asked.

'It won't be,' I assured him. 'No one's that unlucky.'

But it turned out that he was. We were on duty on what was forecast to be an unusually hot bank holiday weekend. And poor old Nicholas was about to do something even more ridiculous.

## 2

# My Name Is Michael Caine

A craggy but friendly face greeted me as I arrived at my locker and got kitted out at the start of our next shift. It was Caddie, the old-timer who'd taken me under his wing when I'd joined Red Watch four years earlier as a super-keen and hyperactive eighteen-year-old. He'd watched me throw myself at every job at a hundred miles an hour. He'd watched me run when it would have made much more sense to walk. And he'd stepped in to help me make the grade. More than twice my age, he had this ever-growing mop of unruly grey hair. He had sharp, deep-set eyes and a military air. And he'd been a tough teacher. He'd never let me get away with a thing. But over time he'd become a great pal – even though over time he'd become a grumpy old sod as well.

'Why the hell are we here on a beautiful day like this? By rights I'd be fishing up at Picklescott. There's a carp there with my name on it,' was his opening gambit.

'A carp called Caddie would be quite a sight,' I said.

'Better than a carp called Windsor,' he said testily. 'I blinkin' hate bank holidays.'

With that he disappeared upstairs to see if White Watch had any tea on the go. We were both early. There had been precious little traffic on the roads that holiday morning in August. Summer bank holidays tended to start on the quiet side. But they normally got busy in the end. Send hundreds – or probably thousands – of hikers, bikers and horse-riders out across our beautiful, tinder-dry county and you can expect a fair few fires to catch as discarded cigarettes and smouldering barbecues do their thing. Send all those people home later on in an awful lot of cars and you can expect a fair few accidents as well.

'Morning, Malcolm. We expecting to be busy?' Next to arrive was Nicholas, the exact opposite of Caddie in the keen-ness stakes. He was the way I'd always been and still was: desperate for the tannoy to call us out. He wanted things to happen so he could prove himself in as many situations as possible. I understood exactly what he was thinking as we got ready for the parade that signalled the start of every working day. He was right to be full of enthusiasm and he reckoned he did know his stuff. So what could possibly go wrong?

The call came in much earlier than we'd expected. We'd seen White Watch get dismissed, been read our notices for the day, drunk our tea and got the net up for a bank holiday game of volleyball. A typically violent, largely anarchic and surpris-ingly high-scoring game was underway when the 'Attention!' call was made. For the second day shift in a row we were sweating cobs as we piled on to the fire engines and headed out on to the road.

We were on our way to a pretty major car crash – or a road traffic collision as they were desperately trying to get us call them back then. It was the kind we got a lot of amidst the blind corners and high hedges of the country roads in Shropshire. As usual some idiot had been overtaking where he shouldn't. He'd slid in between two law-abiding drivers when he'd swung his wheel to get out of the path of the farm truck that could have killed him. The other two drivers had braked sharply, swerved wildly and crashed to a shuddering halt. Three further cars had got caught up in the mess when they too had screeched on to the scene far too fast. The initial call told us that there were no fatalities but a number of casualties needing to be cut out of the wreckage. In the meantime the entire road was blocked, so until we got there to pull the wrecked vehicles apart and clear some space, the county would be facing a major traffic jam.

'Is it too much to expect that the driver who caused it got his car damaged the most?' Caddie asked from the driving seat as we made our way over one of Shrewsbury's nine bridges and left the town behind.

'I think you know by now that life's not like that,' said Joe grimly from the passenger seat.

'He probably got nothing more than scratched paintwork,' added an equally cynical Pete, on the back seat. He was a wiry man with fair, close-cropped hair. His moods could go from gloom to joy at the flip of a coin.

'I bet he drove away and left everyone else to clear up his mess,' agreed Caddie. 'I hate working on bank holiday Mondays.'

I flashed a glance at Nicholas, squeezed between Pete and me on the vehicle's back seat. It didn't look as if we were going to have many laughs today. We seemed to be surrounded by the grumpiest old men in Shropshire.

I tried to cheer myself up by looking out across the countryside as we picked up speed. The height of the fire engine puts you well above the hedgerows. From there you can see so much further than most motorists. And what we could see then was glorious. It was shaping up to be a beautiful summer day. The sun was already high in the sky and a warm haze was building up to make things even more perfect.

I looked down as we passed a wide and sparkling stream.

The water was brackish and brown on the edges. It seemed crystal-clear in the middle where it swirled faster over the rocks. Just across from us an old wooden bridge spanned the water. The air, as we dipped down into a hollow, was moist and cool. The scent of rich green moss seemed to envelop us. Up front I knew Caddie wanted to be fishing in a stream like this. I wanted to be swimming in it. My mind drifted to all the murky streams my pals and I had built dams in as kids. I recalled the hours we'd spent out in the fields on summer days. I thought back to the fireflies we'd watched, the ants we'd tracked and the frog-spawn we'd tried to collect. I've never quite got that thing about Yorkshire being God's Own Country. Surely Shropshire is even more glorious. Its rambling, rolling fields and hills could make any heart soar. We've got hidden hollows, ancient copses and any amount of incredible history. Our rocks are as old as time. Our villages are picture-postcard perfect. We've got grand houses born in the riches of the wool trade. We've got tiny, tumbledown cottages that look good enough to be photographed for the top of any biscuit tin.

I came back to reality with a bump – literally – as the fire engine lurched round a sharp corner then came to a halt. I stuck my head out the window to see what was going on. Not much, was my first impression. The road ahead looked like a long, thin, outdoor car park. At least half a mile of cars were backed up there. None of them looked to be going anywhere soon.

'Looks like everyone's having a party, the lucky blighters,' Caddie muttered as he swung us to the right.

And as I looked closer it was clear that he had a point. The cars might be still, but the drivers and passengers were anything but. All the way ahead of us windows had been wound down and doors were wide open. The lucky few drivers with sun roofs were smugger than ever. Was it wrong to be having a picnic on the grass verge near a car crash? Not really, if there's nothing you can do to help. So lots of people were doing just that. Deckchairs had come out of the boots. Blankets were laid out on the grass. Car radios were playing and footballs were being kicked around. To my left I saw a couple of people who had cracked open their Thermos flask and were enjoying a nice cup of tea. I felt myself smile. This was 'make-do and make-the-best-of-it' Britain at its finest. Other nations might have come to blows, but here a distinctly jolly atmosphere was in the air. With a bit of luck, even Caddie and Pete might cheer up and stop thinking the worst.

Joe gave a few toots on the horn to get people out of our way, then we headed down the wrong side of the road towards the accident scene. A police car was parked up ahead of us, just behind two ambulances.

'OK, lads, you know the drill,' Joe said as Charlie parked the engine near the impact zone. The emergency tender, that day driven by Martin with Woody at his side, was right behind us and we all climbed out and hit the ground at almost exactly the same time.

Joe strode over to talk to the police while we gave the scene the once-over.

Then we got to work. It was automatic. We needed a hose-reel pulled off in case the cars involved burst into flames. And I'll be honest and say that explosions like that happen in Hollywood far more than they have ever – *ever* – happened on my patch in rural Shropshire. We set up a tool dump and coned off the scene to stop some other idiot from speeding in from the opposite direction and making matters worse. Then we got to grips with the casualties in the cars themselves.

RTAs like this can be second nature. We train on this kind of thing all the time. We do endless drills for it on the parade ground. And we face it out in the field on a regular basis. So there wasn't a great deal of talk as we did what had to be done. We didn't need to discuss any clever new strategies. That day we hadn't stumbled across any unusual problems that would have to be solved. We simply got on with the job in hand. Each of us had a different role to play. And as we did so, Nicholas became more and more desperate to prove that he could fit into this well-oiled machine and do his bit.

As a relative newcomer, I could empathise with him. I'd been there myself, so I knew that after the craziness surrounding Bradforth's rescue he would be eager to prove his worth. I watched him dart around the scene like a bluebottle with big fat fire boots on, hell-bent on contributing. And I wasn't alone.

'Beardsmore. Over here,' Joe barked after a while.

Nicholas was at the boss's side in an instant, keen as a puppy. I felt myself grin. He was exactly the way I'd always been. Exactly the way I still was, to be honest. I just hid it better now.

'I want you to make all the vehicles safe,' Joe said. 'You understand what you have to do?'

'Yes, sir. I'll get on it straight away,' he said.

The happy combination of a bluebottle and a puppy hurried off and got busy. It wasn't the most complicated thing in the world. When cars are messed up and mangled in a crash we make them safe by disconnecting their batteries. The last thing you want is for any stray electrical sparks to hit spilled petrol or fumes. If the cars haven't been too smashed up in the crash, we do our best to keep their batteries and engines intact. We use a small 10mm spanner to disconnect the terminals so they can be reconnected when it's safe. The cars that are clearly smashed beyond repair get rougher treatment: we cut their cables in two using enormous bolt cutters. Those cars will never be needing their batteries again, so there's no problem destroying the whole kit and caboodle.

'Hey, Mal, give us a hand with this will you?'

Woody distracted me by asking me to help drag a rogue metal bumper on to the grass verge. I forgot all about Nicholas for a while. Until I heard Joe roar out his name again.

'Beardsmore! What the blazes are you doing?' he bellowed.

'Making the vehicles safe. I've done four already. Am I not going fast enough?'

I looked up. Our newcomer had clearly decided not to take any chances. There were no delicate spanner jobs for Nicholas. He'd got the bolt cutters in his hands and he'd been severing battery leads with relish. He was poised to cut through the fifth but stopped. 'Anything wrong?' he asked, confusion suddenly replacing enthusiasm on his face.

There was a long, painful silence. If Nicholas was a blue-bottle crossed with a puppy, then our lean and lanky boss Joe had turned 100 per cent into a goldfish. He was standing stock-still, his mouth opening and closing soundlessly as he tried to find his next words.

When he found his voice, he didn't take any prisoners. He yelled out with a roar: 'You're only supposed to be making the vehicles safe that have been involved in the accident. Not the ones in the blinkin' queue!'

We all looked up and over. And that was indeed what Nicholas had done. With their owners elsewhere, watching us at the scene, sunning themselves on the grass verges, or chatting to others further back up the road, Nicholas had gone from one parked car to the next, methodically working his way up the line, opening bonnets and permanently disabling their batteries while no one was looking.

'I thought you meant . . . I thought you meant . . .' he began, realisation hitting him like a brick from space.

'Oi – what have you done to my car?' came a yell from a motorist who'd suddenly returned to the scene only to realise he wouldn't be moving any time soon.

'I just – I just—' began Nicholas again.

'My battery leads! Oh my God, you've cut my battery leads!' cried another returning motorist.

'But, but—' Nicholas mumbled, before Joe bundled him away and took him behind the fire truck for what sounded like the biggest bollocking of all time.

The rest of us finished releasing the last trapped casualty before trying to appease the crowd of drivers who had discovered that their stay at the roadside was going to be extended by several hours.

A few moments later, Nicholas headed back to join the rest of us. It seemed as if the happy puppy of an hour ago had been given a smack on the nose – and bearing in mind Joe's volcanic temper, I'd not have been surprised if that had happened for real. 'Sorry, guys,' he muttered, unable to meet anyone's eyes.

'It's all right to be keen. It's not all right to be stupid,' Dave told him, trying to be helpful. 'That's one of the many unwritten rules that they don't teach you in training. You'll not do something like this again, will you, son?'

'Not in a million years.'

'Then you've learned your lesson. You'll be OK.'

'I'm an idiot,' Nicholas said.

'Yes, you are. But it could have been worse. You could have done this at the station on a drill. Do that to my car and it'd be a long time before you walked again. You'd certainly never have children.'

The rest of the clear-up took about an hour, much of which was taken up with apologising yet again to the four newly stranded motorists and their families. We helped a couple of them get transported to town and made sure the others were sorted with their respective breakdown companies. Then we began our own clear-up and began to re-stow all the equipment we'd used on the various vehicles. It was then, I think, that Dave first thought of it. His mood, as it so often did, had changed. The grumpy old man was about to become a comedian.

'Nicholas, you know what you just did,' he began.

'Yes,' said Nicholas grimly.

'Well, you—' Dave stopped, breaking off in annoyance. 'No, that's not right. Give me a minute.'

Nicholas flashed me a look. I shrugged. Who knew what Dave was up to now.

'Nicholas, I've got it. You know what you just did,' he said a few moments later.

'Yes,' said Nicholas ominously.

'You went too far. You were only supposed to blow the bloody doors off!' he roared in his best Michael Caine accent. And while his impression wasn't that good, it didn't stop the rest of us from repeating the line about a hundred times on the way back to the station.

'I wasn't thinking,' Nicholas said again and again along the way.

'Engage brain before all else,' he was told every time.

'And keep your sense of humour,' was the advice I'd have given him if asked. Because he was going to need it.

On the way back to the station we came upon a broken-down

car pulled halfway on to a grass verge outside of the little village of Hanwood. The car's bonnet was up and a smart, unhappy-looking couple were leaning in to the engine with puzzled looks on their faces.

'That's one Nicholas did earlier,' the whole crew shouted out in unison.

The jokes were still flowing ten minutes later as we hit the camber and finally turned into the station yard. Caddie pulled us past our own parked cars as he drove the engine into the appliance room. The Michael Caine impressions rang out again when we went up to the mess room for a cup of tea after cleaning all the equipment we'd used and re-stowing it.

'Have I really got twenty more years of this?' Nicholas asked me, ruefully, when the shift was finally over.

I gave him a sympathetic smile. 'They'll write books about this one,' I said.

# 3

# Space Dust

∞

It was the last Saturday in August and the good weather was back when I left my house at the start of our next set of day shifts. I'd bought the two-bedroom terrace for £15,000 a couple of years after joining the Fire Brigade. Mortgage rates had gone through the roof – hitting something horrific like 16 per cent at one point. But I was convinced I was on a good, safe wage so I was happy to ride it all out. I had plans for the place as well. I had a small building business on the side, doing all sorts of work on other peoples' homes. One day, when I had the time, I intended to do the same on my own place. In the meantime, I was in my early twenties, living on my own across the road from a great pub, with a couple of decent takeaways two minutes away. I'm not sure that life could have been much better.

'Hey, Windsor, get out of my backin' way!' came a roar as I climbed out of my car in the station yard and stood peering at what looked suspiciously like a new chip in the windscreen. I raised a finger and moved even more slowly. Arfer, the first real cockney I'd ever met, had transplanted himself to rural Shropshire about twenty years ago. He'd lost none of his London accent. Or his streetwise manner. He was a lean and fiery man in his late forties, as fit and fast as anything. Once you knew what he could do, you'd trust him to get anyone out of any kind of fix. But at first glance you might have some doubts. Although tall, he had a bit of a hunch. His greying, greased-back hair was thin and wiry – probably the result of too many years smoking and drinking. Right from the start he'd reminded me of Fagin from *Oliver Twist*. On his days off he ran a removal company with one of the other firemen, but I wouldn't have been too surprised if it turned out he had a gang of urchins helping him pick a pocket or two as well.

'I'll run you down if you don't backin' move!' he yelled again. So at last I backin' moved so he could get parked up alongside me.

The two of us were in a narrow gap between the battered old builder's van that our Station Officer John drove and the jet-black Ford Capri that was unaccountably cherished by one of the other lads, an old-timer called Simon. When I'd joined the watch four years ago I'd had an HB Viva that hid its woeful 1159cc engine under flared wheel arches, Rostyle wheels and a host of other flash-looking accessories. A lamb in wolf's clothing, I always said. I had upgraded from that fast, buying a third- or fourth-hand Cortina, which I'd then driven into the ground. Now I was the proud owner of a white 1600 BMW with Alpina stripes. I loved that car, though not as much as I loved my pal Caddie's motor, a 4.2-litre Jag I'd got some serious speed out of when I'd borrowed it a couple of times to impress a few girls.

As the whole of Red Watch knew, my ultimate dream was to own that blue straight six BMW 323i with the whole body kit on it. One day, I told myself. Give me a few more years of working for the Brigade and doing my own building jobs on the side. I'll save hard. I'll get there.

As I gave my windscreen one final look, Arfer strode past me and disappeared into the station. In those days we worked an eight-day rota system: two days on, when we worked nine till six, then two sessions of working six at night till nine the following morning, then four days off. This was the first of our next set of days. I was almost always early, so I sometimes got a quick cup of stewed tea from the off-going watch upstairs before heading down to the lockers to get uniformed up alongside all the others. But as always before the start of a shift I needed to know where I was working. As station manager and Sub-O respectively, John and Joe were in charge of sorting that out. They divided up all the jobs and worked out the positions we'd be holding on the appliances. Every position in the Fire Service comes with a number. When I'd been riding on the water tender ladder for the road accident on the bank holiday, I was number four. That meant I was sitting behind the driver on the back row of the cab, and if we'd been going to a fire rather than an accident I'd have worn breathing apparatus. The driver was always number two, and the jockey tended to be number five – squashed in the middle of the back row with his own specific responsibilities on a shout.

A year or so ago I'd passed my tests and exams and qualified as a driver for the WRT (water tender) and the WTL (water tender ladder) – the two big trucks that most people think of as 'fire engines'. I was therefore eligible to occupy the number two position on those appliances as well as any of the positions in the back cab. Everyone on the watch liked to be in the driver's seat – me most of all, because I got travel sick in the back, especially when it was hot and stuffy or when the driver got particularly enthusiastic on the bends. But there would be serious ructions if someone got to be the driver for more than one shift in a row.

'We're on the WTL – Woody's driving, so hold on to your hat!'

Charlie, rushing past me to get upstairs, was yet another of the larger-than-life characters on Red Watch. He was in his mid-thirties, a little over ten years older than me. At five foot seven he was easily one of the shortest of us on the watch. He was also on his way to becoming one of the widest.

When we first met, Charlie was always giggling. These days he was always eating. He was obsessed by food and talked about it constantly. There was no story, no joke and no tragedy that couldn't be embellished by a description of what he'd had for tea on the day in question. He talked about what he'd eaten, what he intended to eat and what he dreamed of eating. On his days off he travelled to food fairs all over the county. He did a lot of exercise, otherwise the only way he could have put out a fire was to sit on it. To his credit, he laughed a lot too. Charlie was a great pal of mine.

I glanced past him up at the rider board that stood high on the white breezeblock wall at the bottom of the stairs. Our names were on rectangular metal tags. I remembered how proud I'd been, at eighteen, to have one made up for me. Getting your shiny nameplate made up for the rider board was a clear sign that you had arrived. Taking your name with you when you retired was the ultimate souvenir. And there my name was, right below Charlie's. With Woody up front alongside John, and Charlie, Dave and me in the back we'd be ready for anything. But would I be ready for Woody's driving?

I soon found out. The answer was no.

The call came through in the late afternoon. It had been one of our best summers in years and this particular Saturday the sun was blazing down and the temperature had shot up since the morning. There was next to no breeze and it was humid as hell. So all in all the last thing anyone wanted was to run around and get kitted up for a shout. But you can't argue with the fire call. One minute we'd been upstairs in the mess room, downing pint glasses of squash, emptying the biscuit tin, having a crafty cigarette and flicking through the papers. The next minute we were slamming against the pole, shooting down to the ground floor and piling on to the appliances ready for the off.

'This sounds like it could be interesting,' John shouted as he opened up a map on the front seat.

It certainly did. We were on our way to a suspected chemical incident on the outskirts of Ludlow. I was unusually quiet in the back of the appliance as we left the station. I wasn't nervous – not about the job, anyway. I was always up for a new challenge. The chemical training we'd done a while ago had been a real-life boy's own adventure as far as I was concerned. I'd enjoyed learning about chemicals that could turn into an impromptu bomb and how they could be detonated. No, what worried me was Woody's typically enthusiastic driving. He clearly wanted to get us to Ludlow in record time – which meant swerving round one slowing motorist after another, alternating between hitting the accelerator and the brake so often he could have worn a hole in his shoes. It was my worst nightmare.

Over the years I've done everything to kick my travel sickness. Most of the time, I managed. When we had rear-facing seats in the back cab, I twisted around so I could face forward. I gazed out of the windows. I tried to get fresh air flowing when we hit warp speed or slammed round yet another corkscrew country lane.

But that hot and sweaty day it wasn't only Woody's wild west driving I had to fight against. It was the new Chemical Incident Suit I had to wear on top of all the other clobber. Having struggled into my usual fire kit, then the CIS, I had to top it off with the full breathing apparatus set. The chemical suit was hilarious – or it would have been if I hadn't been feeling so sick in it. We'd had a good old laugh about them when they first come in for testing. The Fire Service had clearly decided to go for a one size fits all approach – which meant that the suits were blinkin' huge. Their template fireman was clearly eight foot tall and weighed at least forty stone. The suits were a violent shade of yellow – another negative point when you're feeling sick putting one on. Then there's the claustrophobia. With all the layers – which include a tight hood and Velcro straps around your neck and your usual fire helmet – you're trussed up worse than a chicken. You're totally enveloped.

So what happens if you throw up?

I thought I was about to find out as Woody did the full James Hunt routine on the last few bends before we reached our destination.

If I'm sick, I'll drown, I thought. If I'm sick, where will it go? What do they do in space?

I tried to focus on an imaginary spot on a horizon I couldn't see. I tried to ignore the muffled voices of the others as we lurched to the left, the right, and back again.

And I have never, not ever, been so pleased to get to the scene of an emergency. Dangerous chemicals? I couldn't have cared less. I'd have jumped on moon rocks just to get out of the rollercoaster cab.

Funnily enough, we were presented with something that resembled a moon rock when we arrived. A couple of Ludlow police officers and a member of the public were standing looking uneasily at a sizeable mound of cloudy white crystals on the grass verge of a lay-by. The crystals were giving off occasional puffs of some mysterious, hazy white smoke. As I jumped out of the engine in my vast yellow chemical suit, I must have looked like an alien myself. The space dust on the ground looked like my natural terrain. But what the heck was it?

'There's a specialist team on its way from Harwell,' the police officer said. 'They've got the right equipment. They can analyse it on the spot, by all accounts.'

'Where's it come from?' Woody asked.

For some reason we all looked up. Space really did seem the most likely answer.

While we waited for the specialists we set about cordoning off the area – and the next part of my nightmare began. I was no longer worried about being sick. Now I was in danger of being poached.

It was hotter than anything inside my new, bright yellow, chemical-suited world. My sweat created its own endlessly re-plenishing eco-system. It misted up my visor and ran down my back. Where the heck were the specialists? And what would they tell us about this bizarre pile of unearthly mate-rial? It appeared to be shifting, slightly, in the grass. Parts of the edges were breaking off. It looked like the sort of thing a mad professor or a James Bond baddie might have created. Spectral smoke was rising up from it and drifting in the gentle afternoon breeze. Could the fumes kill us? Would more of the white stuff rain down from the skies at any moment?

'All right, lads. You look like you're ready for the worst.'

I turned around as quickly as my vast yellow suit would allow. A dark blue Cortina had pulled into the lay-by. Out of it climbed a man I vaguely recognised as one of the retained fire-men from Ludlow. I didn't know his name, but I remembered him as a cocky, arrogant type with a strut of a walk and a real know-it-all attitude.

'The experts are on the way,' he was told as he approached the officer in charge.

And he laughed.

'We don't need to wait for them, and none of you need your stupid suits,' he declared. Then he walked under the cordon, strode up to the pile of smoking powder and plunged his bare hand into it.

'Are you out of your mind?' Joe yelled at him.

Our retained guy laughed again. 'If you think that was good, watch this!' he said. Then he reached into the smouldering pile of pure whiteness a second time. He picked up some of the crystals. And he ate them.

'What the eff are you doing?' Joe shouted.

Then the man really took his life in his hands. He scooped up another handful of space dust – and threw it at us.

Forget health and safety. Forget words like toxic, caustic or poison. Forget fellowship with your fellow fireman. We were ready to jump him. We were about to pound him into the ground.

'Keep your hair on – it's ice!' he crowed, standing back and looking ridiculously and annoyingly pleased with himself. 'It's from my mate's ice-cream van. He dumps it here every day. It builds up around the refrigerator. And when the weather and the humidity is like this, it steams away like a train for a good hour or two. You've missed your tea and got dressed up like a friggin' banana over a pile of ice!'

Everything felt better on the way back to the station. I'd got out of my chemical suit as fast as I could. It had sat there, crumpled on the grass verge like a discarded snakeskin as I breathed in some fresh country air and tried to cool down.

'Bloody hell, Windsor, you're steaming too,' Woody said as he watched me.

And I was. I was wet with sweat. I could have wrung out my shirt and collected enough water to brew a cup of tea. 'I'm not looking forward to wearing one of those on a real shout,' I admitted.

'Well, let's not tell the others that we got duped by a pile of ice today,' shouted Woody from the driving seat. None of us replied – we knew it didn't matter what we did or didn't tell the rest of the gang. The story would have crossed Ludlow by now. It would bounce across to Shrewsbury faster than Woody could drive. The joke was well and truly on us. We'd be ribbed about it for months.

Nicholas, meanwhile, had spent the whole morning safely revising for his exams in the study room at the station. He was finally off the hook.

# 4

# The Next Big Test

∞

I strolled into the station and took a quick look at the rider board. Then I stopped short. Where was my name? I ran my eyes down the board once more. I wasn't there as one of the five on the water tender ladder. Nor was I on the list for the water tender.

I flashed a quick look around. Thankfully none of the other lads were with me in the corridor at that exact moment. I felt a hint of a blush hit my cheeks. Was I supposed to be on leave? Had I booked some time off and forgotten all about it? If I had, and if the lads realised what I'd done, I knew I'd be ribbed about it for weeks. Maybe for months. Way back in the early spring a newcomer called Robin had transferred in from another station. On one of his first shouts with us he had put his helmet on the wrong way round as we piled out of the engine at a factory fire out east towards Telford. He had noticed, straight away, as you would. He had taken the helmet off and put it on the right way round within seconds. Nevertheless we did endless imitations and took the Michael out of him for it. And we still would, probably for the rest of our careers.

At that moment Robin himself thundered through the open station door. He slapped me on the back so hard I'd have fallen over if I'd not been ready. I'm six foot four and

I towered over him. But what Robin lost in height he made up for in width. He was fanatical about body-building. He spent most of his days off at a gym in town. He'd discovered a rusty old set of dumb-bells in one of our storerooms and worked out with them most afternoons when the rest of us were drinking tea, lying in the sun or catching up on other things.

'I'm on the bleedin' WTL, sitting next to Dodger, who won't shut up for a moment after what happened to Forest on Saturday. What have I done to deserve that?' he said to no one in particular as he stormed on up to the mess room upstairs.

Normally I'd have smiled as he passed. We all did these little assessments when we saw who we were working alongside. Sometimes I'd think: I'm with Jeff or whoever it might be today. It should be a breeze. He'll have all the answers. Other times I might think: Right, working with Howard or whoever it was. Might be tricky. Better get my head in gear in case something kicks off.

But where the hell was I working that day? That's when it hit me. Had I been sacked? Was that why my name was the only one missing from the list? It was 1985 and job losses were headline news every day. We'd had strikes all over town. Sure, we'd taken on newcomers like Nicholas and Robin. But that didn't mean a thing, did it? I wasn't blushing any more as the thought hit me. I was pale. And that was when I saw it.

Malcolm Castle. There it was. My metal nameplate. Not under the WRT, or the WTL. No, I was lined up next to Joe's name on the emergency tender.

I felt my breathing pick up. I was on the emergency tender. John, the officer in charge of Red Watch, had finally gone and put me on the E blinkin' T. I felt like giving a yell of joy. It was the biggest step up since I had qualified as a driver two years ago. It was the one big level I had left to achieve on the watch. There's nothing official about getting moved on to the ET. You don't sit an exam, you don't get a new job title and you certainly don't get a pay rise. But what you get is confirmation that the boss thinks you know your stuff. He thinks you can be trusted to handle yourself – and a whole lot of heavy, expensive kit – on some of the most complex shouts we go to.

'Out my way, lad. No time to stand and stare,' said Simon, one of the other old-timers, as he too pushed past me.

'Morning, Malcolm, can you help me with those exam questions later?' Nicholas asked as he too strode into the station and checked his position on the board.

'Of course I can,' I said, absently.

I looked at my watch. I had a good ten minutes or so before I needed to be uniformed up and on parade for the start of our shift. I flashed a glance into the appliance room to look at the ET and get my brain in gear. The ET gets parked alongside the other main appliances. It is basically a workhorse with room for only two firemen – so you either drive it or you sit in the passenger seat sending messages or reading maps. The vehicle is massively overloaded with kit and mainly goes to rescues – of people, animals, vehicles or a combination of all three. It's needed at road accidents where people might be trapped in their vehicles. It's got a lot of lighting on board so it's needed at a lot of night-time shouts. And it can often be the first of our vehicles to get to any given scene – so if you're on it, you could be in charge from the off.

A lot of the time an ET will turn up to a twin turnout alongside one of the retained crews from a station out in the country. For all their training and enthusiasm, those lads aren't likely to have had as much hands-on experience as us. When that happens they look to the ET guys to make the decisions and take the lead. That's why being on it is such a big responsibility – and why this can bring challenges of its own.

'With great responsibility comes great amnesia' was one of the many unwritten laws of the Fire Service. John's putting me on the ET showed that he reckoned I knew my stuff so well I'd not succumb to that problem. He'd decided I was ready. I was flattered, thrilled, and mildly terrified to get the imaginary stripe on my shoulders and be on the ET at last. But I knew I mustn't show it. 'Look cool, Malcolm, look like it's just another day,' I told myself.

I flashed a sneaky look around. The hall was quiet. I took a gulp of air. I tried to fix an unimpressed, maybe even a bored and cynical look on to my face. You didn't get excited about things like this in the Fire Brigade in 1980s Shropshire. Well, you did. I certainly did. But you didn't show it.

Chewing an imaginary piece of gum, hopefully in the manner of a Shropshire James Dean, I headed up the stairs to the mess room. Most days if I was early for a shift and wanted a sneaky cup of tea I did this at least two steps at a time. That day I walked up slow, steady and controlled. Because I was cool, unimpressed and bored, right? I didn't want to look too eager. I didn't want anyone to know how big a deal this felt.

I grabbed my tea and listened in on all the usual banter up there. Green Watch, the outgoing watch that had done the night shift, had spent most of the small hours out west at a farm where a selection of prize sheep had apparently decided to take up pot-holing and had discovered that what goes down doesn't easily come back up.

'I still can't believe that farmer. Standing there like a statue, refusing to help, and smoking a clay pipe,' one of Green Watch was saying.

'No one's smoked a clay pipe since Roman times,' Simon told them.

'That far west they think it still is Roman times,' was the considered Green Watch conclusion.

Right on cue, shortly before nine, everyone headed downstairs. While we paraded in the appliance room, Green Watch did the same in the muster bay on the other side of the double swing doors. When they'd been dismissed, John, our Station Officer, read the notices for the day and gave us the official take on the pot-holing sheep incident that had taken place in the night. Our conclusion, funnily enough, was that we'd have handled the whole thing much better.

Two minutes later we were dismissed. We got out of our dress uniforms, lockered them up and headed on into the appliance room in our overalls. It was time to do our start-of-shift checks. That day I watched as Woody and Dodger climbed aboard the WTL to check their breathing apparatus sets and other kit. Charlie, as number five on that engine, checked the BA board, the general use torches and the hand-held radios. Martin, as driver, did the 'A routines': checking lights, fuel and general roadworthiness of the appliance before going through the lockers to make sure that nothing was missing. All around me others were doing similar checks on their appliances. And I was about to do my first-ever checks on the ET.

Being on board with Joe, the Sub-O and the second most senior officer on the watch, meant I wasn't likely to get away with cutting any corners. Not that I wanted to. If I was doing this, I wanted to do it right. If you're going to be a bear, then be a grizzly, right?

Over on the ET, Joe and I did our own A routines. Again

that was the fuel, tyres, road lights, blue lights, hazards, radios, torches and all the vehicle-controlling switches. We checked the fuel levels in the generators and compressors we carry in the many lockers. Job done, we moved on to check the fuel in the Stihl chainsaw and circular saw. All the vehicles get a weekly inventory check, so on an ordinary shift like today we ended the checks by doing a quick walk around, looking for any obvious gaps or damaged kit.

'Happy?' Joe asked, having had his eyes on me just as much as on the ET through the entire process.

Had he seen something I'd missed? Had he been testing me? Could I fail? It was too late now. So I nodded. 'Happy,' I said.

He nodded too and we got the logbook from inside the cab, signed and returned it.

As we did so, Martin's deep baritone boomed out. 'Check me lights for us!' he shouted out from the cab of the water tender ladder. One of the others then yelled out that all was well with the brake lights from behind.

'Tea's up when you're ready' echoed through the appliance room. It meant when all of us were ready for the off, in case the alarm rang. But we didn't want it to ring just yet. For this was our cue to head upstairs for a brew.

As usual the mess room was soon full of smoke and noise and newspapers. Our two morning cleaners were busy in the kitchen, sorting out the mess Green Watch had made during breakfast. Years ago we'd had two regular cleaners – a little and large duo called Bev and Babs. They'd loved being two mouthy women in an entirely male world. They had the raciest, dirtiest conversations – and ruled the roost for every moment they were at the station. Cutbacks had seen them lose their jobs a year or so ago. Now we had agency staff who changed all the time – but who still managed to add some spice to our mornings.

'There's not much room, but I'm game if you are, love,' the first of them said suggestively through the hatch as I made my way to the fridge for some milk.

'Always room for a little one,' her pal sang out.

I grabbed the milk, poured myself a big glass and tried to make a joke about tight spaces. It didn't work and wasn't really funny but the ladies laughed like drains. 'I can't stand the heat,' I said, as we always did to them. And so I got out of the kitchen.

Back in the relative safety of the mess room with the rest of the watch, I glanced across at John, the officer in charge who devised all the working positions. He was stubbing out a cigarette as he prepared to take his tea down to the OIC's office on the ground floor. He'd chosen today to test me on the ET. Neither of us did anything to acknowledge the fact as he passed.

I considered edging my way across the room to chat to Joe. I thought it could be useful to chew the cud before we headed out, a lone duo, on a shout. But Joe was lying back, eyes closed, on a battered old armchair by the open window. I decided he wouldn't take kindly to an interruption. So I did what I usually did. I joined the others and got involved in a ridiculous argument with Charlie over his favourite subject: food.

'I tell you, the portions were too small,' he was saying, outraged.

'They were perfectly normal. You all saw me. I cooked everything that was in the fridge,' declared Ben. We each took turns to cook the evening meals on night shifts; Ben was one of our best and most generous chefs.

'Then someone is playing silly buggers with something. Food should cover the whole plate, every last inch of it. When I stand at the hatch I don't expect to see the pattern on the plate. If the main part of the meal doesn't cover it all up, then the gravy should fill in the gaps. If you don't burn your thumb in gravy carrying your plate from the hatch to your table then you've not been served enough. It's that simple,' Charlie was saying.

'And your thumb survived OK?' asked Pete, a full portion of sarcasm in his voice.

The gentle mockery passed Charlie by completely. 'Yes, it did survive. And it shouldn't have done,' he said in all seriousness. He then veered off onto a related topic. To everyone's shock, our weekly subs for food had recently gone up to a record high of £5 a week. We got a fairly decent amount for it, looking back. Two dinners and two breakfasts on our night shifts, two lunches on our days and all the tea and coffee we could drink – which always turned out to be a heck of a lot.

Charlie, though, wasn't happy. 'Five pounds is a national scandal,' he began. 'We're being hit from all sides. We're paying more and we're getting less,' he said. Then he looked darkly at Woody. 'Sometimes I wonder if every penny of our mess money is getting through.'

If anyone but Charlie had said it, Woody would have flattened them. As it was, he merely laughed. 'I've been mess manager for nigh on six years now and not a penny has gone missing. If you want to spend your time chasing tightwads for small change, then be my guest, Charlie-boy,' he said. 'We all take our turn being mess manager and buying the food for the watch. We all see what's spent and what's left over. You're not being short-changed, Charlie.'

'I'm wasting away,' he claimed, despite all evidence to the contrary.

I smiled along with the others. I tried to join the conversation a few times but my heart wasn't in it. Instead, I downed my milk, grabbed a mouthful of biscuits and went over everything I knew about the ET, my mind racing.

I'd cleaned the thing since day one. As the new boy, the jockey, I'd spent hours doing that. I'd been with it in the appliance room while the old-timers were upstairs knocking back the beers and having fun in the station bar. I'd examined and polished every inch of it. I knew how everything worked and where everything on it went. For our exams, I'd even learned how much the kit weighed and where most of it was made. I'd used the kit as well. We all did, doing the endless ET drills in the yard on day shifts and going through as many complicated scenarios as the boss could devise. The basic deal of the Fire Brigade has always been that everyone could do anything – just in case.

Meanwhile, in the mess room, Charlie's attention had turned to Dodger, who he said was eating far more than his fair share of biscuits. Dodger had joined Red Watch a year or so ahead of me. He'd been out on the ET last week, with Pete in the driving seat. Pete was one of our real old-timers who'd seen and done it all. The pair of them had been sent to a three-car pile-up on one of Shropshire's notoriously dangerous country roads. We didn't have motorways in Shropshire so we didn't get a lot of high-speed, single-direction crashes. What we got instead tended to be a lot worse. If I had the choice between something going wrong on a road where everyone is going in the same direction at seventy miles an hour and on a road where two cars are coming at each other head on at fifty miles an hour, I know which I would choose.

Dodger and Pete's call had been what's known as a 'split turnout' with one of the retained crews from Wem, the small market town up to the north of Shrewsbury. Retained crews are sort of paid volunteers. They train up and go through most of the usual assessments and exams. They agree to be on call, and to stay within a set number of minutes of their local station, for most of each week. They're the backup when the regulars are all occupied. On a road incident like last week the retained guys would probably have stepped back while Pete and Dodger used the cutters, spreaders, jacks and props from the ET to slice through various parts of the cars. They would then have helped out as everyone manoeuvred the cut sections to gain access to any casualties.

As it turned out, there'd not been much cutting or spreading on Dodger and Pete's shout. Just a lot of dragging. No lives had been in danger. All the drivers had got out of their own accord, or with the help of the ambulance crew. Dodger and Pete ended up making the cars safe and pushing them off the road to open it up to traffic. Back at the station, they'd bragged about how fast and efficient they had been.

I wish that had been me, I thought as we packed up shop upstairs. I knew I could have handled something like that, even with Sub-O Joe's beady eyes watching my every move. I was desperate for a call to come in so I could prove myself in reality.

But I didn't get one. At ten o'clock the net was put up, turning the drill yard into a volleyball court. We pulled on our trainers and launched at the ball, and at each other, with a wild, brutal abandon. An hour later, with no serious casualties, we had a fifteen-minute mid-morning break to try to get some fluids down our necks. We also piled into the kitchen for cheese on toast at 20p a slice on top of our usual mess money.

Heating that up was normally done by whoever was the cook that day. That day Charlie slowed things down by all but measuring each slice of cheese to check he wasn't getting less than anyone else. I wolfed my slice down, scalded my throat with my tea and then we followed John's call downstairs.

Five minutes later we were all driving out through the appliance-room doors. The good news was that I was behind the wheel of the ET for the first time. The bad news was that it wasn't exactly a live shout. We weren't off to fight a fire. We weren't going to be carrying lovely ladies out of burning buildings. We weren't rescuing wild animals or saving farmers' livelihoods, we'd not had a call to a car crash, a chemical incident, a suicide attempt, a bridge collapse, a trapped child or any one of the dozens of calls we got in any given month.

Instead we were off to spend a happy hour poking round a country house hotel.

'I read a review of this place in the *Star* when it first opened,' Charlie had said after John briefed us on the job. He'd cheered up no end the moment we heard about the visit. 'The food's supposed to be top notch. I think they gave it one of their best-ever ratings. Said dinner was as good as anything you'd get in the best places in London. Said the Full English was the best hotel breakfast they'd had all year – if not ever.'

'Charlie, I hate to disappoint you, but we're not going to test the room service menu,' said Pete as we trooped into the appliance room and got aboard our various vehicles. What we were actually doing was getting a feel for the layout of the place. Big hotels, especially in rambling old buildings, can be a rabbit warren of corridors and stairwells. The guests only see the best of these. Go behind the doors market 'Private – Staff Only' and there's probably a rat run of shabbier routes where the chambermaids and other staff dart around. Throw in a scattering of storerooms – often on each floor – where lots of chemical cleaning fluids lie alongside piles of tinder-dry towels and sheets, and it's a wonder anyone can sleep at night. Our familiarisation trips – otherwise known as 11d inspections – are designed to make things go a lot smoother if disaster strikes. If you can't see a thing in a smoke-filled corridor it's good to remember where it leads – and what kind of hazards might be round the next corner. Over the years we get to go in all kinds of weird and wonderful local buildings so we know the layouts if they catch fire. We've climbed towers, descended into bank vaults and walked through all manner of tunnels. We've toured factories and traipsed around vast new warehouses. And right from the start that day's tour looked set to be a cracker.

'Welcome, gentlemen,' the sharp-suited hotel manager said as various vehicles came to a halt and a couple of dozen pairs of shoes crunched up the gravel on his drive. 'I've asked my assistant Marina to show you around. And we've arranged coffee and biscuits in the ballroom afterwards,' he said.

Charlie perked up at the word biscuits. And we all perked up when Marina approached. She was lovely. About five foot six and roughly my age, her dark suit clung to her body and her dark, glossy hair was tied up neatly on top of her head. Her eyes were warm and dark and small silver earrings flashed in the morning sun. She was wearing a soft, white, open-necked blouse, higher than expected heels and just the right amount of make-up.

'Follow me,' she said, with a hint of a cheeky smile.

'Our pleasure,' we said in unison.

As it turned out, the whole visit was a pleasure. Flirting with Marina and with all the chambermaids we met was

huge fun. Going up, down, round and around the old building was a treat too. Someone had spent big money on this
place. As a part time builder, I was paying a lot of attention to the work they'd done. Loads of conversion jobs were
being done in town and it was good to see how bedrooms
and bathrooms had been squeezed into some very unlikely
spaces here. Charlie, of course, was totally enraptured by the
tour of the shiny new kitchen. And his day was about to get
even better.

'If you've not got lives to save, you're more than welcome to
stay for an early lunch rather than just tea and biscuits,' the
manager said, having rejoined the group at a fire exit at the
back of the property. 'We can't offer much more than a cheese
ploughman's. But it will be on the house.'

'I think we'd all find that very pleasant indeed, thank you
very much,' said Charlie in a huge rush.

'I think you'll find I'm still the officer in charge here,' said
Joe, his voice even gruffer than usual. Then he too smiled. 'But
a modest cheese ploughman's would be most welcome. We'd
be pleased to accept.'

I flashed a look at my watch as the manager, and Marina,
led us back through the hotel to a vast, ornate function
room at the rear. It had just gone twelve. Back at the station
I knew Maggie would be hard at work in our kitchen. She
would be preparing the day's two-course meal. It would be
hot on the hatch for us all at 1 p.m. on the dot. Joe clearly
had the same thought as we took our places at a huge
round table.

'We will have to leave here at twelve-forty at the latest,' he
told the manager decisively. 'We do have another important
appointment at one.'

'So, Charlie, how do you rate their lunches? As good as the

critics made out?' I asked as we walked round the side of the hotel to get back to our appliances.

'It was a very good first impression,' he admitted. 'I'd certainly consider eating there again. But I'd not say those portions were much to write home about. I'm still starving. I reckon I could eat a horse.'

'I reckon you probably have eaten a horse,' said Dodger.

'Well, I certainly hope to be eating something good in . . .' Charlie looked at his watch, '. . . approximately ten minutes' time. Get a move on, Des, or Maggie will have our guts for garters.'

Years ago we'd had two weekday cooks at the station, Betty and Mabel, who had run the kitchen and, in their own way, ruled the station. Those two older ladies had stood, arms folded, in front of a dozen or so big, hungry firemen and asked if we'd washed our hands. They had scolded us for our language – even though they would sometimes let rip themselves. Along with our cleaners, and as the sole female influences in our station life, they had followed all our highs and lows. They had stopped us boasting when we got above ourselves. They gently, cleverly, lifted us up when things got bad.

Mabel had retired first, a year or so ago. Betty had followed shortly afterwards. Now we had only one lunchtime cook, Maggie, who somehow managed to keep order, and cook pretty well, all on her own. She was stouter than either of her predecessors and kept her hair tucked into a cook's hat. She had a heart of gold and was always up for a bit of teasing, but would immediately scold us if we ever crossed the line. That day, little more than half an hour after our hotel meal, she served up a piping-hot liver-and-bacon pie and one of the biggest and richest puddings this side of Charlie's imagination.

At the start of the meal I burned my thumb in the gravy on the pie. Maggie had passed Charlie's portion-control test with her usual flying colours. At the end of the meal I did it again, burning my thumb in the scalding hot custard that covered every inch of a life-threateningly large portion of jam sponge.

'Two full lunches in a row. It's your perfect day, isn't it Charlie?' I said as we polished off the contents of our bowls and sat back in our chairs with big mugs of tea.

'These aren't words anyone says too often. But, Windsor, you are absolutely right,' he replied with a smile.

Immediately following the meal, and with stunning illogicality, we were back on the volleyball court to play until the end of the dinner hour. No one got badly injured, threw up or had to be carried to Casualty with killer cramp, and at three-thirty John said we could knock off for the rest of the afternoon. Most of us used the time to get on with all sorts of other business. John himself spent his spare time running his ever-growing building company and said he had invoices to do. A couple of the guys went out into the yard to wash their cars, Martin was in the workshop welding a pair of wrought-iron gates, one wanted to work on his tan and climbed up onto the flat roof of the storeroom to catch some precious rays. Last but certainly not least, Bob, who had unaccountably decided he wanted to learn to play the bagpipes, was walking up and down the appliance room giving 'Flower of Scotland' his best shot. The noise was bloody atrocious.

I left most people to it. I helped Nicholas with his revision as I'd promised. Then I sat back and decided to stop looking at my watch. I didn't manage it. In truth, if I checked my watch once that afternoon I checked it a hundred times. But time passed and we didn't get as much as a whiff of an emergency call. My big moment on the ET didn't arrive. 'It's not the end of the world,' I told myself when our shift finally ended. 'There's always going to be another time,' I said as I headed home. But was there? Little did I know that the following day everything would go wrong.

# 5

# 'Watching Windsor!'

The drills had begun so well. We did training drills out on the station yard all the time. In the week we did them every day shift when we weren't on a shout. We did 'bullshit drills' where you do the same mind- and sometimes body-numbing tasks again and again. You carry the same ladders, roll out the same hose-reels and use the same equipment over and over. You do the drills up and down, round and round and inside and out. It has to be that way. Bullshit drills work because they ram home your ability to do certain jobs. The aim is to make them second nature, to get to the point when you can do them in your sleep.

Not that we can go to sleep out on the drill yard, of course. When I'd joined as a green-as-grass teenager I knew all eyes were always on me in the drills. The others wanted to be sure I knew what I was doing. They needed to know I could handle things if the bad stuff hit the fan. I'd swallowed the pressure and taken the scrutiny as part of the job. I'd looked up to the old-timers like Caddie and Pete and Ben and Simon and dreamed of the day when I too would be under the radar on the drill yard. Four years on, I knew that wasn't how it worked. The old-timers were under almost exactly the same amount of pressure. The Fire Brigade was no place for sitting on your pro-verbials. You have to be tested – and to prove yourself – each and every day. Maybe the old-timers were under more pressure than the newbies, I thought now. They had to prove they were still fit and fast enough. The Fire Brigade is a great life. But no one ever said it was easy. As I was about to find out.

'Squad! Squad! 'Shun!' Joe roared in his avalanche-creating bellow. Then he began a stream of instructions that would make no sense to anyone listening in from the other side of the fire station wall. To an outsider, even the words they could understand would seem to be in the wrong order. But we knew what was meant.

'From the right in fives number. Crews number. Number one crew, your drill will be to ship the standpipe and supply the appliance with two lines of two lengths of seventy-millimetre hose. Then I want two jets supplied with three lengths each. One from the ground, playing on to the BA chamber roof, and one played into the first-floor window of the tower from the 10.5 ladder.'

He paused for a quick breath. There was always more to come.

'Number two crew, your drill will be to slip and pitch the 10.5-metre ladder and extend it to the second-floor window of the drill tower.' There was the most minuscule of pauses. 'Any questions?' An even more minuscule pause. 'Right then, squad, fall in two paces to the rear of and facing the appliance. Fall in.'

We turned smartly to our right. We doubled away to end up behind the appliance.

'Number one and number two crews . . . Get to work!' And so we did.

We turned Joe's words into actions. We moved fast. And afterwards, when he'd said half a dozen Girl Guides could have done a better job, we got ready for phase two.

Scenario drills are the ones I like the most. They're pretty much what it says on the tin. The officer in charge describes a scenario. It can be simple and deadly – or it can be long and extremely complicated. It can also change, as the exercise goes on. Just like real life. Once the command is given, we work as a team. We tackle the situation using a combination of knowledge from all the bullshit drills and the applied common sense we're supposed to have as a given. It's normally the Leading Fireman or the Sub-O in charge of the operation. But sometimes one of us is given the lead. It's a good way to show everyone what it's like to stand back and control an incident.

The last one we'd done had been a cracker. A building was said to be on fire behind our fire station – which rose to three storeys once its attic space was included. The drill had it that the only access to the fire was over the roof of the station. We'd sweated like pigs carrying some of the equipment we needed up the ladder on to the roof and hauling the rest up by ropes once we'd got there. That part of the job done, we'd prepared to fight the fire – until the OIC of the drill had his say and bowled the googly.

'An unconscious and injured casualty has been located on the ground beside the burning building,' Joe yelled. A bit of yelling, a bit of mindreading and a bit of common sense helped us adapt our strategy to that, the way we would in real life. Two of us had carried on fighting the fictional fire while two others got down to the training dummy that had been laid out ahead of us. We didn't have a stretcher, so we tied him to a single extension of a short extension ladder using a bacon roll knot. Then we carried him back to the appliance where we had an imaginary ambulance waiting.

Today things looked to be even more interesting. One of

the local scrapyards had given us a car to play with. It was an old Ford Escort that had seen better days – and it was about to see a lot worse. We always had fun with those cars. If it was a model anyone was interested in, it would be liberated of any useful spare parts. Then, on the drill ground, we'd cut it up, squash it down, bend it, force it, and eventually destroy it. We prised those cars open and pulled them apart. And then, when they were totally ruined, we'd get the scrappy back to take them away.

There were seven of us waiting for instructions that day. And there was an unexpected face on the drill ground.

'I'll take over from here,' John said as he strode out to join us. I felt my breathing pick up. The scrapyard car meant this drill was all about the ET. Last week John had decided I was ready for that challenge. Now he wanted to make sure.

'Bring round the ET and the WTL,' he began. We raced to oblige. I was on the ET with Des, the others were on the water tender ladder. We parked them, as directed, alongside our scrapyard car.

We then lined up to hear the scenario. It was short and to the point. 'We have conscious casualties in the driving and passenger seats. The only safe access is through the roof of the car. Remove the casualties. Get to work!'

We got the chocks out to stabilise the vehicle before all else. With imaginary people trapped inside, and with lots of big machinery about to be deployed, you don't want it going up, down, backwards, forwards or anywhere else.

'Get the zip gun – we'll cut a roof flap,' Simon called out. The zip gun is an air-operated hammer-and-chisel that cuts slots out of sheet metal. Our aim was to cut a D shape in the car roof that would be opened along the straight edge and folded back like opening a can of beans.

'Get the roof off completely,' John yelled when we were half-way through the task. That meant cutting through the car's A, B and C posts – the vertical posts that support the roof. Our Fag Lucas cutters would do that trick. They needed connecting up and as I was closest to where the hoses were stowed, it was my job to do it.

It wasn't the most complicated thing in the world. I'd worked on this kit loads of times on the training ground and out on a shout. Plus, for every time I'd used or seen this kit in action, I'd probably cleaned it ten times more back at base. I'd polished every inch of it on long, boring sessions in the appliance room. I knew everything about it. I knew, for example that you use a locking collar between the hose and the tool. I knew that you screw the collar up to lock the two pieces together – because as soon as the 700-bar pressure of the hydraulic oil comes through something very explosive and damaging could happen if you don't. And how do you screw the two pieces together? 'You do it with ease,' I'd have said half an hour earlier. 'I can do it in my sleep,' I'd have claimed. But I couldn't do it that day.

'Here we go,' I said to myself. I got the parts together, the peer pressure was on, John's eyes were boring through my skull – and the blinkin' things wouldn't connect.

'OK, one more try,' I muttered, under my breath. I pulled the hose and tool apart and brought them back together. There was nothing. No click. No fix. I twisted and I even forced them. Nothing.

'Come on, Windsor!' I heard the yells from the rest of the group. I swear I could hear some giant clock ticking above my head. I tried again. I pulled them well apart, as if that might help. I swung them back together. Still nothing. I was failing and I was panicking. So what the hell was wrong?

'Windsor, we need this done!' a voice yelled out from the other side of the car.

'Ready!' another voice yelled as his part of the jigsaw of jobs was completed.

And still it all continued to go pear-shaped for me. What I know now – and what I did actually know then – was that the collar had to be screwed back into its rest position before a connection would hold. Only then can you screw it forward to create the seal. That day the collar was fully forward at the start of the drill. All I had to do was move it back, connect it, fix it and get on with the job. It's the easiest, simplest thing in the world. It's hardly any different to pumping up the tyres on your car. But for some reason I couldn't see it that day on the drill ground. For some reason I acted like a total, first-class, blinkin' idiot.

'Get it sorted, Windsor!' came a cry yet again. I knew by then that I'd already made a right royal balls-up. Could I recover from it? I tried over and over. I tried fast and I tried slow. I did everything – except screwing back the collar and doing it right. Everyone saw it. Including John, the man who mattered most.

'Rest!' he bellowed. The one word I had learned to dread the most. The word that always meant someone was getting it wrong and needed bawling out. The whole drill came to a stop. But John gave me the nod to carry on. Everyone was looking as I carried on failing and flailing.

'Simon. Get over there. Show him what to do.' Simon was at my side in a second. He took the supply hose from me. He held on to the collar. He undid it the few turns it required. He connected hose to tool with a satisfying – and humiliating – click. He screwed the collar to lock them together. Job done.

'Drill continue!' John gave the call. The oil flowed, the cutters worked and we began to slice through the first of the roof posts. John yelled a selection of other instructions at us as we progressed. He changed the scenario and made us tackle other hazards in the hour and a half we worked on that old car. After my stupid mistake I did everything spot on, first time. I did my tasks fast as well, as fast if not faster than all the others. But the back of my skull no longer ached. I could sense that John was no longer looking at me. He'd been watching like a hawk when I screwed up. He was looking away when I got things right. Blinkin' typical. Blinkin' disaster.

'Knock off! Make up!' John barked when he had finally seen enough. We moved to re-stow the way we would on a job. The appliances had to be ready for a real shout.

'Drill completed, sir! All gear stowed!' Simon reported.

Then we got the word we all wanted. 'Dismiss!'

We slammed our way towards our appliances. We pulled off our fire kit and pulled on our overalls. Then we did the herd of hungry elephant impression and thundered up the stairs to the mess room.

'Maggie's done a real rib-sticker of a fish pie!' cried Charlie as we skidded towards the serving hatch. He was suddenly the happiest man in all Shropshire.

And if he was the happiest, I was the opposite. John had been testing me for the ET. He must have had doubts about me and I'd made them real. That balls-up on the drill could have set me back a year. Maybe longer. I was in a daze over lunch as I tried to work out if I could salvage the situation. One half of me wanted to go downstairs and raise it with John – to explain why I'd messed up and why I'd never do it again. But why had I? In truth I had no idea, it was just one of those weird things when stuff goes wrong. Anyway, the other half of me wanted to bury the story, to keep quiet about it and not risk drawing any extra attention to it. Maybe John hadn't been paying as much attention as I'd thought. Maybe he hadn't really been testing me.

That half won. One of the many unwritten rules of the Fire Brigade back then was 'least said, soonest mended'. We joked about everything and everyone. But we didn't talk about important things. We certainly didn't admit to any weaknesses.

'What's the matter with you, Malcolm? You barely ate your lunch. No seconds at pudding either. Something wrong with my semolina? I'll have you know that jam was home-made.'

Maggie had sidled up to me as I stood by the window look-ing out over the drive towards the road. I flashed a quick glance around to check no one was close enough to hear. Plenty of people were. But they all seemed to be busy in their own crazy conversations as usual.

'I'm fine,' I lied, keeping my voice low and trying to smile.

'You always have seconds,' she persisted, as she stood back and put both hands on her hips.

'I wasn't hungry.'

'Don't be soft. You're always hungry.'

'You've got an answer to everything,' I said.

'So what's up? Love life giving you gyp?'

'My love life's fine.'

'Well, your building work is doing OK because I know Mrs Bagge at number forty-two has spent a week trying to get you to give her a quote on her new kitchen cabinets.'

'I will give her a quote. I've been busy, that's all.'

'And being busy is what's bothering you?' Maggie looked rightly sceptical.

I sighed. There was no point in hiding things from Maggie.

She was always ready to mock us, joke with us and shout at us. But when push came to shove she saw us as family. A couple of years ago, when Howard had been on holiday in Malta, there had been something in the news about a British man drowning in a hotel pool there. 'One of my boys could be in trouble,' she kept saying. She'd worried every day till he showed up for his first shift back after the trip. She cared. So I told her. 'I just screwed up out on the drills. I forgot something really simple. I made a right royal fool of myself.'

'So?'

'So, I think John was testing me and now he's not going to roster me on the ET again.'

'ET? Like the alien on the bicycle?' she ventured.

'Maggie, you know full well what the ET is. You've worked here long enough.'

'Well, it's good to see you smile. And do you know what else I know?'

I didn't ask. It was clear she would tell me anyway.

'I know that you're not half as important as you think you are. I doubt that anyone gives a flying fig what you did on the training ground today. When did you get to think the world revolves around you, Malcolm Castle? King of England, are you, all of a sudden?'

This time I didn't just smile, I laughed. Maggie always knew how to bring us down to earth. 'That's better,' she said, as she gave me a flick of the tea towel and headed back to the kitchen to get her coat and head off for the day.

The rest of us got on with our afternoon. And I soon snapped out of my gloom. 'John knows what I can do,' I told myself. 'And if it takes me a year to get back on the ET, then it takes me a year. There will be plenty of fun to be had in the meantime.'

I'd certainly got that last part right. Because at the start of our very next day shift we got the sort of crazy call you can't prepare for. Once again it was the kind of thing you never hear about in training.

We were about to rescue an invisible woman.

# 6

# The Tartan Slipper

The initial message was short and to the point. It was coming up to ten in the morning and we had been called to an address out on the southern edge of town. 'Person trapped in toilet,' we were told. That was the message written out on our copy of the docket and passed over from the watch room when the call came in.

To be honest, it wasn't that unusual. We got calls like that a lot. We still do. It's normally kids who get stuck. It's amazing how often they accidentally lock themselves in the bathroom and can't – or won't – come out. Sometimes they might have snapped the lock or done something silly to jam the door. Other times they're just being, well, kids. I've talked through enough bathroom doors in my time. I've stood on enough ladders trying to negotiate with a six-year-old through the frosted glass of a bathroom window the size of a car number plate.

We make a lot of promises in these hostage situations. 'Open the door, matey, and I promise your mum won't mind,' I say. 'No one's cross with you, not even a little bit,' I fib. 'Come out and you can have a seat on a real fire engine,' I plead. And, last but not least: 'Of course we can break the door down without doing too much damage.' That's normally the lie we tell to the poor kid's mum.

It wasn't a kid that warm and airless late September day. We didn't have far to go and we weren't in a hurry. You can't die by being trapped in a toilet – unless there was something else very bizarre going on. So we didn't need to use the siren. But we did make decent progress, with the good, early morning drivers of lovely Shrewsbury getting out of our way wherever possible to see us through the town.

We rumbled past the picture-perfect Lion Hotel where Charles Dickens had stayed when he was in town to give lectures at our Music Hall. We shot past some of the town's hidden lanes, narrowest streets and easily overlooked pedestrian passageways – 'the shuts' as they're called locally. If we'd had time – and if we'd not done it a million times before as kids – we might have sniggered at some of the street names, Grope Lane being a firm favourite and Gullet Passage top of the list for places where restaurants may or may not want to open. We got a wave from a couple of people some of us knew. And we got an envious look from Norman, the copper, who was directing traffic with an incredibly bored expression at a set of broken traffic lights on the far side of the English Bridge.

The house we were looking for was in a Sixties-style suburban development with wide streets and masses of easy parking.

'That's the place. Number sixty-two as I live and breathe,' said Ben, from the passenger side of the cab. He was the most senior fireman on that day's team.

The front door to the house opened as Dodger parked us up. A huge redhead in her mid-fifties came out and gave us a surprisingly cheery wave. She was wearing a vast blue denim skirt topped by a thick, tent-like black jumper. She beamed out an equally big, wide, toothy smile as she stomped down the front path. Every spare inch of the garden was covered in bricks and wood, rubble and rubbish. 'She's in here – my daughter. She's been there for hours. Hours!' she said as we hit the pavement and joined her.

'What exactly has happened?' Ben asked. His eyes, like mine, had appraised her and were now giving the house and garden the same once-over. It looked like a building site. Which the mother immediately confirmed.

'Her name's Nancy. I'm Sue. She lives here with her husband. I live across the way with my Stuart at number seven. Sue's having her house turned upside down. The pair of them are getting work done on every room. It's taking them forever. I told them they should get help. They don't listen. They say they can do it on their own, but they can't.'

Ben tried to stem the tide of words. 'And what happened today? Your daughter is trapped inside?'

'I came across to drop off some frozen meat from our freezer before going to work. A pair of rump chops for their tea. I told my Stuart we'll never eat them ourselves. They're hard up, poor loves. I like to help. Anyway, soon as I got into her kitchen I saw her foot.'

'Her foot?'

'Well, I saw her leg and her foot.'

Ben flashed a quick glance at the rest of us. His massively outdated Seventies moustache twitched. Was this something to smile about? Was it a wind-up? Or a freakish medical emergency?

'Where, exactly, did you see her foot?' he asked.

'In the ceiling,' she said, as if this was the most natural thing in the world.

Still not entirely sure we weren't about to star in some hidden camera skit like *Beadle's About* we followed Sue into the house. Nicholas was working with me, and the pair of us were right behind Ben as we crossed the half-plastered hall with wires hanging off all the walls and made our way into a surprisingly big kitchen at the back of the house.

'There's her foot. Up there,' Sue declared with pride.

And yes, up there in the far corner of the ceiling was not only a foot but an entire leg!

'Nancy, my darling, the Fire Brigade is here,' Sue shouted.

Nancy, unseen above us, gave a loud wail. Her foot, wearing a natty tartan slipper with a large floppy pom-pom on top, started to wobble alarmingly.

'The bathroom is up there, above the kitchen,' Sue continued, barely lowering her voice. 'They're working on the floor or the ceiling or something. It's not safe. I told her it wasn't safe. Nancy, my love, didn't I say it wasn't safe?'

Nancy wailed again.

'They keep the toilet roll on a hook on the back of the door,' Sue went on.

'Mum! Don't!' came the cry from above.

Mum waved the objection aside. 'Nancy, my sweet, it's all perfectly natural. You'd gone to the little girl's room. You were sitting on the loo, weren't you? When you leaned forward to get the toilet roll?' Sue turned to us. 'She put her weight on a loose floorboard. Or it might have been a rotten one. Her foot went right through it.' She looked back up at the slipper. 'You got stuck, didn't you, my darling?'

There were more wails from above. And I have to say, the 'little girl's room' didn't seem to be the most accurate description. Sue, as I said, was a very large lady. She probably weighed more than most of us – and we're all at least six foot two. The size of her daughter's bare leg suggested that this sort of thing ran in the family.

'When did it happen, Nancy?' Ben shouted up at the slipper.

Sue jumped in and answered for her. 'It was hours ago. Her husband had gone to work. If I'd not come round with the pork chops she could have been there all day. Sitting on the toilet floor, all on her own.'

'And you can't pull your leg back through, I see,' Ben said. Then he turned to the lady's mum. 'Have you been up there? Have you tried to help from upstairs?'

'Can't get in,' Sue stated with something close to satisfaction. 'The door's locked and Nancy can't reach the lock. Will you need to go up and break it down?'

There was another moan from above. And then, in the lowest of whispers, Nancy spoke. 'Mum, I've hardly got any clothes on,' she said.

'She says she's only got a short nightie on! I think she's almost as naked as the day she was born!' roared her mum, in a voice loud enough to wake the dead, and certainly to reach the neighbours.

The foot jiggled around anew. 'Stop it, Mum!' she begged. Then, after a pause, came a question. 'Mum, how many of them are down there?'

Sue did a head count. 'There's three in the kitchen and I think a couple more outside. They all look very nice young men,' she said.

The wails from above grew even louder. Ben's moustache was definitely twitching now. The rest of us were biting our lips as we took a closer look at the ceiling. It was time to go to work. And however odd all this seemed to be, it was important to be kind.

'Nancy, I'm Ben Elliott from Shrewsbury fire station. I'm here with two of my colleagues, Malcolm Castle and Nicholas Beardsmore. We're going to get your leg free. And we might be able to do the whole thing from down here so you don't need to worry about us coming up there. Give us a minute to get a ladder and to arrange our equipment.'

The piercing wail had turned to a softer moan. That had to be progress.

Out in the street we discussed the task as we got some kit together. I did a lot of building work on my days off – most firemen had second jobs or spivs back then. I knew that the floorboards round toilets could get pretty manky over time. In a more modern house things might not have been so difficult to sort out. Chipboard floors and plasterboard ceilings are much easier to break up. Nancy's home had traditional floorboards and a lath-and-plaster ceiling. When Nancy's leg made its bid for freedom and aimed for the kitchen below, the laths that held the plaster in place had split and bent downwards. When she tried to pull her leg back up through the hole, those laths closed up again like a set of jaws. The same thing had happened, though to a lesser degree, with the floorboard itself. And the end result was that Nancy's leg couldn't be freed without assistance.

'We're going to have to cut the wood away with a handsaw and a hacksaw blade,' Ben explained quietly to Sue when we were back in the kitchen assembling the tools.

'They're going to use a big hacksaw, my darling!' Sue shouted up helpfully.

The soft moans had gone. The wails were back. And I had a feeling that in a moment's time Nancy wouldn't be the only one who felt the day had taken a turn for the worse.

'Nicholas, my son, this is a job for you,' Ben said, proving my point entirely.

I let myself smile. I'd dodged the bullet. Sometimes I forgot I was no longer the new boy on the watch. I forgot that I could stand back while Nicholas got up close and very personal to what had to be one of the larger legs of Shrewsbury.

There was a look of pure trepidation on his face as he picked up the saw and moved towards the target.

'Cup of tea, boys? Cup of tea, Nancy, my darling?' Sue, oblivious to the embarrassment factor, was busy making herself at home. She clicked on the kettle, and pulled a handful of mugs out of the rather grimy sink. 'You got any biscuits, Nancy, my love? All the boys down here look as if they'd like biscuits. I'm sure the others outside would like something too.'

The wailing got louder. And then it stopped. It stopped suddenly and totally. It stopped the precise moment the kettle clicked off. Because at that exact moment Nicholas began the job.

The sound of sawing echoed through the silent kitchen. Nicholas was in the zone. With one hand on our victim's bare leg, he began to saw away at the wooden ceiling. Sawdust and small chunks of plaster fell to the floor.

'The more I cut, the more I could see,' he said grimly, once we were back at the station.

At the time, in the woman's kitchen, the rest of us could only stand there and wait. What, or how much, would this job reveal? And when would it end?

'Can you hold still for me, Nancy?' Nicholas instructed as he began a new set of incisions. Sue, meanwhile, had turned back to the kettle and was distracting us all with our tea.

'You can't beat a nice cuppa, gentlemen,' she said, as if all this was the most normal thing in the world. Another piece of ceiling lath fell to the floor. A whimper, this time, from above.

'Would you like some butter?' Sue asked me, out of nowhere. I looked at her blankly.

'In my tea?' I asked, unable to quite put my brain in gear.

'On her leg,' she snapped.

'Oh, of course. I understand.' I turned to poor Nicholas. 'Would some butter on her leg help?' I asked.

I got a look I don't think I'll ever forget. 'You know what, Malcolm, I don't think it will,' he said. His face, which was almost always smiling, looked horribly strained.

Not that Sue seemed aware of the tension. 'How are you feeling up there, Nancy, my darling?' she shouted. She was unstoppable, unshockable, this woman. She was easily distracted as well. 'Oh look – it's Anita and Samuel from across the road. Little Patrick is with them. I'll just pop out and tell them what's going on.'

Alone in the kitchen I gave the ceiling a proper scan as Nicholas nipped and tucked away with the hacksaw blade. The last thing we wanted was for the whole structure to collapse. That would have been one way to finally meet Nancy in the flesh, as it were. But not a good way. I prodded the stress points of the ceiling with the back of a chisel and reckoned we were safe for a while.

'Not long now, Nancy,' Nicholas said. His voice sounded almost cheerful, though his face remained horribly strained. He was reaching right up through the lath and plaster ceiling now, right up by the top of Nancy's thigh. Once more I thanked my lucky stars I was no longer the jockey of the watch. 'OK, your leg's a bit scratched and you're going to have some bruises on it. But I think we're clear now. I don't think there's anything in the way any more. Are you able to pivot a bit? Can you pull yourself forward and lift your leg up and out? Or do you need some help from someone down here?'

I glanced out of the kitchen window as those last words came out. Sue was some distance away now, standing hands on hip, chatting happily to a growing group of goggle-eyed friends and neighbours.

'Don't know if I can move. I'm cold and my leg's numb,' Nancy said from above. Her foot did move after a few moments. But it didn't pull itself up through the hole.

'Is there anything you can hold on to? Anything you can pull yourself up with?' Nicholas asked. There was more than a tad of desperation in his voice. If I was a betting man, I'd have put money on him being well on the way to full-scale panic.

'I'm trying. I'm trying,' Nancy said. There was some bumping and scratching going on as she pulled herself forward somehow. This was followed by a loud thump and the entire ceiling shook. Plasterboard, wood chippings and dust rained down on the kitchen. Nicholas visibly flinched.

'Nearly there! Nearly done it,' Nancy said. She shook her leg wildly. And her slipper fell off.

It was odd, looking back. But that felt like the poor woman's final indignity. The plush, purple shoe landed with a thud on the kitchen floor. Nancy's bare foot loomed large above us. It was fleshy, not bony. Her nails were painted bright red.

'One more pull, Nancy, and you'll be free,' Nicholas said, more in hope than in judgement.

And then he was proved right. Suddenly Nancy's foot started to move. She must have found the leverage to lift it up and out through the hole.

'I'll call your mum,' I said, and went out to drag Sue back to the house. She didn't come alone. Anita, Samuel, Little Patrick and several others were hot on her tail. It was like one of those parties that end up in the kitchen.

'Oh thank you, thank you so much!' Sue said as we all watched Nancy's foot disappear for the final time. 'Are you OK, love? Can you stand? Can you open the bathroom door? I'm coming up.'

The rest of us stood sheepishly in the kitchen surrounded by neighbours as we waited for a first-hand report from above. No one looked up through the hole Nicholas had cut in the ceiling. Well, Little Patrick did, but his dad whacked him round the head and sent him back out into the street.

'We cannot thank you all enough. You're the very, very best,' Sue was saying five minutes or so later when we'd re-stowed our kit in the engine and were getting ready to leave. 'I can't remember whether she's had her tetanus. She must have done as a little girl, mustn't she?'

'It's a long time since she was a little girl,' Nicholas muttered ungallantly, that strained look back on his face again.

'You should take her to the doctors to get the cuts and scrapes looked at, just in case,' Ben said.

'You will forgive her if she doesn't come down to thank you in person?' Sue asked, serious for the first time since we'd met her. 'It's stupid, and I told her she was being a baby, but she doesn't want to face you. None of you. I swear I don't know what's going on in that head of hers. She says she's embar-rassed, for some reason.'

'She's no need to be,' Ben said, not entirely accurately. 'But we totally understand. We're only glad we were able to help her out of her little, well, fix. We'll be saying good day now.'

We were surprisingly quiet on the way back to the station. Poor old Nancy hadn't had the best of mornings. It would have been mean to take the mickey out of her. So in the weeks and months ahead we'd take the next available option. We would continue to take the mickey out of poor old Nicholas instead. His happy horse and his Michael Caine incident on bank holiday Monday were almost forgotten. We'd talk endlessly about his 'new girlfriend' instead. 'Look, that's Nancy,' we'd say every time we saw a fuller female figure in the street. No idea if we ever got it right. But that woman with a limp we saw once in Abbey Foregate? The one who turned on her heel and ducked into the doorway of the chemist as soon as she saw the fire engine? That had to be her, didn't it?

# 7

# Tragedy on the Road

❧

I was there again. My nameplate was on the board and on the emergency tender. It was ten minutes before the start of our next shift. My balls-up on the ET drill had been forgiven or forgotten. I said thank you about a hundred times in my head. John still trusted me to do this job – all of it. The imaginary stripe was back on my shoulder. And surely, today, we'd get a call and I could prove myself for real.

Better still, I was paired up with none other than good old reliable Caddie – the old salt who'd been my mentor since I'd first joined the watch four years earlier. I was on the board as the driver, Caddie was number one in the passenger seat. That role gave him official responsibility for the appliance, even though the responsibility was seldom wielded and nine times out of ten ET crews managed incidents on a two-man committee basis.

The morning had begun the way they normally did. John had read out the notices after we'd gone on parade at the start of the day. He'd told us about the standing corn fire that Green Watch has been tackling for most of the night. He told us that one of the retained crews had been called to a pub fire in one of the hamlets out east. He told us that if the morning was quiet, one of the other crews would be going out on hydrant duty. Then he told us to go upstairs for a cup of tea.

I shovelled in the sugar and got in a tussle with Pete for a newspaper that was lying on the arm of one of the sofas. And then everything changed. The phone must have rung down in the watch room. Simon, on duty down there, took the call, wrote down the details on the official, duplicating pad and then pressed the button for the tannoy. The alert tones sounded. The vital first word cut through every conversation: 'Attention!'

You could sense the anticipation in the air in that split second. The need to get as much information in the shortest possible time. What was the shout? Who and what would be needed? Where did we have to go?

'ET to road traffic accident on A5, West Felton.'

Everyone moved. It was only Caddie and me who would be off on the shout, but we'd not be going down to the appliance room on our own. I skidded across the parquet floor of the mess room first, slammed down the pole and was racing towards the ET within seconds. Caddie was inches behind me – and the others were right behind him. The doors to the room were opening in front of us. We'd recently had a new system installed that rolled them up automatically when an alarm call came through. The other lads were there in case one of us got injured on our way to the ET and had to be replaced. They were also there to give a final visual check as we set off – and to help replace any kit that had been taken off by someone cleaning it, practising on it, revising with it or using it for any other strange reason.

There were no last-minute injuries or crew switches that day. There was no missing kit. No problems whatsoever. So this was it. I prepared myself for a host of different things in those last seconds before leaving the station. You have to. And you know one key thing about car crashes. In the Fire Brigade there's an obvious and well-known rule about them. In simple terms, it states that if cars crash and the people inside can get out on their own, then they will. If they need a little help, then passers-by or the police will give it. If there's more of a problem, then the ambulance crew will step in. If we get the call, then things must be serious. We'd got the call.

'You're ready for this?' Caddie said as we slammed the cab doors shut.

I was. And I was determined to do everything right. 'I'm ready. This is what I want to do,' I said.

He nodded. 'Well, we'll be doing it as a team. We'll be just grand.'

Sitting in the driving seat, I fired up the ignition and got into gear. I felt like a giant, up high and behind this wheel. We eased forward, round the yard and out into the road. My eyes were everywhere. They scoped the road ahead, behind and all around. My first challenge was to get us to our destination in one piece. The ET was a tough old bird to drive – and it felt a lot harder on a live shout than it had ever done in practice. It was massively overloaded with kit. It was a lumbering, almost uncontrollable tank. It was the size and weight of a lorry – but it had the braking capabilities of a Citroen 2CV. Fire Brigade folklore is rife with tales of badly taken corners and ill-judged, disastrous emergency stops. I eased the wheel through my hands as we rolled through the crowded streets of Shrewsbury. I liked driving. I always felt comfortable in charge of the other appliances. I picked up the pace as we headed downhill and out of town. I had to make everything work on this big beast as well.

Traffic eased off once we crossed the River Severn – and the drive was easier because we knew exactly where we were going. Caddie, tapping his big boots in time to a song he was humming, didn't need to get a map out or direct me. The crash we'd been called to had taken place near a pub. And most of us knew exactly where all the local pubs were.

'There she stands,' Caddie said as the Old Forge Arms came into sight. We passed it on our right, rolled around a wide sweep of road and then reached the scene. At least half a dozen cars and vans were lined up, blocked by the accident and clearly unsure whether to wait or turn back. We passed them on the right-hand side of the road. Up ahead were the other emergency services – a police car and an ambulance. I slowed as we approached. We recognised some of the people, but none of them were smiling a greeting, and there seemed to be a heavy calm over the whole scene. You get to recognise that calm in this job. It gives you clues about what's ahead.

'Hello, gentlemen,' Caddie said as we climbed out of the cab and approached the others.

'Sad business,' was all the police officer said. He was a tall, bony man with sharp eyes and a suspicious manner. I'd worked alongside him at plenty of shouts over the years, though his name escaped me that day.

'What are we looking at then?' Caddie asked.

Ahead of us, just past a small junction, was a selection of vehicles. Up front, facing us, was a large tractor that had clearly been pulling a huge trailer. Behind it, and half alongside it, was a heavy lorry. In the middle, firmly in the middle, was what must once have been a small, fast car.

'The trailer is full of sugar beet. Packed solid with it and hard as nails,' the officer continued. 'It was heading east, as you can see. It was on the point of turning into the lane right there.'

'Perfectly normal. Nothing unexpected,' said Caddie.

'The car driver wouldn't agree,' we were told. 'He'd not

expected it, or he'd not seen it, or some combination of the two. Marks on the road tell us he slammed on his brakes. He skidded a heck of a way. Then he hit the trailer side-on.'

We nodded. That kind of thing happened all the time on country roads like ours.

'And that's when he got really unlucky. That lorry was coming down the other way. It must have come round the curve the exact same moment. And he didn't have time to see or expect anything from that angle. He smashed right into the side of the car. It happened faster than you could blink. He hit the car side-on as well. He hit it with the full length of the lorry.'

That time we didn't nod, we winced. Looking at the scene, it was obvious what had happened next. That small car had been sandwiched between two very big, very solid objects. It was an awful lot smaller now.

We were about to step forward to examine the scene in more detail when the retained crew from Oswestry arrived. We waited till they were on the ground then repeated the police officer's briefing.

'And the driver?' Caddie asked as we stepped forward. We already knew what the answer was likely to be. If he was alive, but trapped, we'd have been taken straight to him. If he was alive, and had walked away, we'd probably not be there at all.

'He's still in the car. He won't be going anywhere,' we were told. It confirmed what I'd guessed right at the start. It was my first time on the ET. And someone had died.

'Right, let's take a closer look,' I said, catching Caddie's eye and sensing his permission to take joint command. The ambulance crew greeted us in a subdued fashion as we approached them.

'It would have been over in an instant. He'd not have known

a thing, far less felt anything, the poor bloke,' the first medic said quietly.

At that point a shout and a cry and sounds of commotion came from the ambulance behind him. We heard someone gasping. Half-swallowed cries. Then silence.

'It's the driver from the lorry,' said the medic. 'He's in shock. He's never been in a collision before. He's not quite with it at the moment. He's taking it pretty bad. The tractor driver is over in the police car. He's shook up too. Beautiful day, isn't it? No one can believe it.'

We left the ambulance and walked towards the centre of the crash site. There was less actual damage than you might have expected. The lorry and the full trailer were as solid as a couple of brick walls and there was barely a mark on them. The car, on the other hand, had been pushed in on itself like some kind of concertina. There was glass and broken lights and a bit of other debris on the ground. But not as much as you'd have thought. Everything had ended up going inwards, not out. And that, we soon saw, included the driver.

'It's a terrible sight. It's a terrible thing,' the police officer muttered as we stood and looked down at the car.

The driver's whole body had been crumpled in the collision. If his small car had become a lot smaller, then so too had he. Most of his body was out of sight, under and amidst the twisted metal of the front of his car. Everything below chest height was obscured. The one thing we could see clearly was his head. And this was something I'll not forget. It too had been squashed. His skull had somehow lost its shape. His eyes, the poor man, seemed to have been forced on each side of his head. There was very little visible blood. But that made the extraordinary deformity seem even more unreal. The man looked like an angelfish, poor guy. Even his mouth was open.

It was wide, square-shaped. It had been pushed and held that way by the impact. The man had been frozen in the moment he had died.

'It must have been so fast. He can't have known a thing,' I said, trying to persuade myself, the way you do.

'Always best that way,' said Caddie. 'Let's get to work.'

The men on the retained crew set up their tool dump, made sure the cordons round the scene were in place and stood to one side waiting for further instructions. I certainly felt the real responsibility of being on the ET that day. It didn't seem that long since I'd been the new boy watching what everyone else did. Now all eyes were on me. It was time to free the man's body.

As the driver was dead we didn't have a clock ticking in our ears the way we do with a live and injured casualty. But there was still a great deal to do. With so much impacted metal we'd struggle to get close to the body, let alone to get him out with due dignity.

I headed round the side of the ET to start unloading the kit we needed. I took my time and paid attention as I unclipped the first of the latches. Simon, one of the real old-timers at the station, still got ribbed over the time he opened the back locker too fast and saw the sliding tray come flying out of its own volition. It knocked him for six, by all accounts – in full view of the retained crew and a whole host of rent-a-crowd passers-by who were lined up watching every moment.

Thankfully there were no problems as I eased the compressor out of its compartment. It was heavy, some thirty kilos. And it was unwieldy. Once that was in place we began the huge task of forcing the lorry and trailer apart. We used the hydraulic spreaders and rams to gain access. We used the Tirfor winch to pull the lorry backwards, then got the hydraulic cutters to cut the car apart when we had the room to do so.

Most of the tools we used that day made a huge amount of noise. But I still remember it as a quiet job. It almost always is, when someone has died. If there's to be any banter, any black humour to get us over the shock, it will come later. At the time, at the scene, it's a place of work. People deserve as much dignity as we can provide.

'Well, I think this is as far as we need go for now,' said Caddie after about ten minutes of hard labour. 'There's room to move. There's access.'

He called over the ambulance guys and the police. We had a doctor on the scene as well, to officially certify the driver as dead. With that task completed it fell to the local undertakers to come forward with their plastic coffin. They were smart, respectful men, not particularly old. They travelled to scenes like this in an ordinary, nondescript transit van. The traditional hearse is only for funerals. Most of the time the bodies they transported from scenes we attended would be going to the mortuary, leaving the powers that be to investigate exactly what had happened.

Despite the casual nature of their van, and the fact that the terrain at the scenes they attended might require them to wear wellington boots, the undertakers always showed respect. They wore dark, smart suits. They must, sometimes, have shared the black humour that gets the other emergency services through the bad times, but they never showed it at the scene. They certainly didn't that warm, late summer day when they laid the plastic coffin on the ground in the space we had carved out between the vehicles.

Having cut, spread, twisted and pulled enough metal apart, Caddie and I helped lift the man's broken, bloody and terribly misshapen body into the box. We bowed our heads as the lid closed on this gentleman. I then looked away as the undertakers lifted the coffin and carried it to their van. Caddie, I saw, was staring at the ground as the short procession passed. It took them a while to secure everything in the back of the van. Then, with sober nods and the low growl of a surprisingly well-tuned engine, they were gone.

'Right, let's finish this,' said Caddie.

The mood was different now. I can't say it had lifted. The shadow of a tragedy never quite disappears from a scene. And you do have to be ready for the unexpected. One of the other crews had a story about a similar car crash long ago. They'd been faced with a male casualty who had died within moments of their arrival. They'd done just what we had done: secured the scene and made it safe, then created access to the body. An hour or so later, when the undertakers had gone, they started to clear the wreckage so the police could reopen the road. It was then, with one carriageway open, that the man's wife drove by. Her car had been in the line of traffic held up by all the work. She'd had no idea that her husband's car had been involved. She had no idea he was dead.

'It was shock and grief like you've never seen it,' the leading fireman had told us. 'She stopped when she saw the car. She came to a stop right there on the grass verge. She came towards me at a run. Then she fell apart. She was on the ground. She was fighting me to get to the car. She seemed to be sure that he had to still be there. She thought she could see his body still in it. She wouldn't believe that he had gone. She fought so hard. A terrible, terrible day.'

And then he'd said something else, that older, old-school fireman with the military air and the dark, knowing eyes.

'I'd been leaning on my shovel when she came out of the car.

I was smoking a cigarette. I must have looked like I didn't have a care in the world. Her husband had died. He was the father of her children. And I looked as if I didn't care. I'll always be sorry for that,' he'd said very quietly.

Caddie and I stood back for a few moments as the police examined the driver's seat and bagged up a few items. Now that there was room, more pictures were taken. When that was done we got the retained crew teed up and got to work. We used our kit to cut through and separate the last parts of the car so it could be dragged onto the low loader and taken away. We helped make sure the lorry and the trailer were safe to be moved. We cleared up the remaining debris and then the police decided that the road was ready to reopen.

I remember something else from that day. As the cars started to file by, I remember the wide, sad eyes of drivers and passengers alike, unable to resist staring out at the scene. But what I also remember was the silence. Even with the traffic, there seemed to be a hush in the air.

There was a fair bit of banging and crashing as we re-stowed the kit on our vehicles. Clips snapped shut, locker doors were slammed, motors were turned on and off. But through it all there were moments of peace. We were in the heart of this lovely county. The hills rolled away smoothly on either side of the road. Nature was alive, where so recently there had been death. Bees were humming and buzzing around. Truly beautiful birdsong rang out every now and then. Far above us a lone buzzard patrolled the sky. The occasional burst of wind sent rustles through the hedgerows and the nearby trees.

I slammed the final locker door closed on the ET and turned to the retained crew. 'Thanks for everything, lads, see you again,' I said, as we got ready to head our separate ways.

'Well, that's your first time on the ET crossed off your list,' Caddie said as we left the scene and headed east.

'It's not one I'll forget. The poor guy. The worst luck, the worst timing you could possibly imagine. And all over in an instant,' I said, staring at the road ahead.

Caddie didn't reply. We sat in silence as I eased us round the one-way system into the centre of town, past the red sandstone castle, past the railway station and back towards our station. Then, as I turned the vehicle into our yard, he said the four short words that meant everything: 'You did well today.'

# 8

# The Saddest Day

Death stalked us that autumn. Within days of losing the car driver on that lonely stretch of country road we were called to a fire at a modern house over in Radbrook Green. It's a nice suburb, mainly made up of modern homes, to the southwest of town. We were starting out on the first of our latest couple of night shifts. The call had come through right at the start of our duty. It had been one of those perfect, early autumn afternoons. Now the sun was hanging long and low in the west, a glorious ball, with the richest of colours. It looked set to be a beautiful evening. But it would turn out to be one of the saddest nights of my whole career.

It hadn't begun that way. All the usual joshing and joking had gone on as we waved our sarcastic, mostly one-fingered goodbyes to Blue Watch and took control of the station for the night. By quarter past six we'd been on the parade ground doing the first of our drills and looking forward to an amazing fireman's dinner to follow. Ben was back on kitchen duty and was talking of a massive fish pie with a mountain of mashed potato and vast piles of fresh veg. The good old Thoms, the couple who had once run the frozen-food shop on our corner, had been passing through town earlier on. They had come in for a chat and left a tray of home-made shortbread for Blue Watch and a tray for us. Amazingly, our tray hadn't gone missing in action during the afternoon. We'd enjoy eating that after Ben's much-talked-about pie. Although it wasn't his signature dish; that was a super-sweet rice pudding, thick as anything, with a sticky crust and infused with spicy poached apples, pears and all sorts of other goodies. Ben was the example I always gave when I told friends and family how surprising firemen could be. After years of jokes, he'd recently given in and shaved off his military moustache. But he'd not lost his army roots. He was stiff as a board, the ultimate gruff sergeant major type. In his time off he coached rugby, followed football and went racing. And oh boy did he love to cook.

We loved to let him, of course. Each watch operated a rota that made sure everyone did their fair share, and on each night shift two of us would cook the dinners and the breakfasts. I did a mean mixed grill when our budget allowed. If the money in the mess tin was there, I'd do the works: sausages, bacon, black pudding, tomatoes, eggs, onion rings, baked beans, chips – and lots of everything. The food was always wolfed down with enthusiasm, but Ben's nights were the ones everyone looked forward to the most.

I swear I spotted Charlie looking up longingly at the kitchen window as our second drill came to its close. I swear he sniffed the air. But we never got to see what Ben had cooked up that night. The alarm came through shortly before seven. And it was serious. It wasn't just a house fire. There were 'persons reported'. That meant every second would count.

We were off the drill ground in a flash. Both appliances were mobilised. In total, nine of us were on board the pair of them. Both sirens were carving through the air as we left the station, powered past the traffic and headed out.

I was on the rider board as number three on the WTL and Dave was number four, so he would be at my side when we fought the fire. As we'd had the persons reported call – meaning people were thought to be trapped in the burning building – we had more to do on the short journey. We were the two on our appliance who needed to pull on our full kit, including breathing apparatus, as Simon steered the engine to the address.

'Nicholas, get down out of the way,' I said as I swung the mask over my head, checked my torch, axe and other extras. The whole point here is to be ready to hit the ground running. You need to be 100 per cent ready for anything. These are the life-and-death jobs, the ones that really got the blood pumping.

It wasn't hard to spot the house in question as we rolled into a wide, well-maintained cul-de-sac. This, very clearly, was not a false alarm. Blue flashes from a police car and an ambulance were slicing through the early evening light. A huge crowd of desperate, panic-stricken people had already built up in the street. Despite what looked like the best efforts of the police, several people were right up against the front wall of the house we were heading towards. A ladder, clearly far too short, had been pulled up below the bedroom windows. People were running around, ferrying small, domestic buckets of water to the fight the blaze. Apparently in defiance of the commands of the police, several of the neighbours had broken through a mini cordon and were throwing water ineffectively at the walls, doors and windows of the house. A garden hose, not long enough to be of any use, was lying in the middle of the street where it had been brought then abandoned. Its water drained uselessly down the opposite camber of the road and into the gutter. Everyone was shouting, crying, yelling orders; it was like driving into a wall of noise. The house looked every inch the ordinary family home. At the same time it was obviously the scene of an extraordinary tragedy that was unfolding before our eyes.

'This is it – get going, you two,' Simon muttered as he hit the brakes. Dave and I jumped to the ground the moment we slowed. We ran round the side of the engine and began pulling off the hose-reels, ready to sprint up the short path to the front door. Behind us, Simon had jumped out of the engine and started opening up the valves in the pump bay to supply water to our hose-reel. Within seconds the water would flow.

'Malcolm, Dave – your tallies.' Nicholas was setting up the breathing apparatus board at the front of the engine. He took the tallies – the plastic identification badges on our BA sets – and slid them into the clear Perspex slots on the board. Then he got a pen out and marked up some other facts. The tallies and the BA board list vital information: our names, the pressure in our cylinders and the exact time we began breathing the air. It would be Nicholas's job to do the sums and work out how long we could stay in the fire and when we should be coming out.

Dave and I had the job of going in to fight the fire, to look for casualties and to do everything we could to get them out safe – and fast.

From the corner of my eye I saw the team on the other appliance getting ready for their own tasks. John and Joe were engaged in a hasty, shouted conference with one of the policemen on the scene; as soon as they gave us the nod, I turned towards the house and acknowledged the thumbs-up from Dave. It was time.

The noise from the fire was shockingly loud, even as we pushed against the front door. It opened straight away. That was the first good thing that happened that night. It would pretty much be the last.

Dave was slightly ahead as we went inside. There was that unique combination of smoke, fire, darkness and light all around. The colours and the sounds were intense. So was the heat. This fire had taken hold horrifically fast. And it was clear that the very structure of the house would soon be in serious trouble.

Ahead of us was the staircase. Flames engulfed the bottom of it. Although it wasn't entirely burnt yet, it was obviously well on its way. When patches of smoke and flames cleared for an instant we could see that whole sections of the wood were burnt through. There would be no way upstairs from there. And we soon found out that upstairs was exactly where we needed to go.

Teams from the other engine were tackling what looked to be the worst of the blaze from outside the house. They had dragged their hose-reel round the side of the building and were firing water through the broken windows at the back. Dave and I headed out to report on what we'd seen and find out what anyone knew about the occupants. The information hit us straight away, from all sides.

'She's up there! In the bedroom! She was at that window right there. She got the kids out from it. Two of them. She dropped them both down to us.'

'This was the only ladder we had. It's nothing. It's too short. But it was just about enough.'

'She said they couldn't get downstairs. She said the smoke was too thick. She was trapped in the bedroom.'

'She was in a terrible state. She was screaming. But she couldn't breathe.'

'She lowered the kids down to us. She did everything she could.'

'But she fell back. We were shouting at her. Screaming. Begging her to come back to the window.'

'We went everywhere to find a longer ladder. We did everything we could to get up there. But the heat was like nothing you've ever known. It was so awful. We're so very sorry.'

'We've not seen her since. We can't get up there. We can't get in. She's there in the bedroom still. She's right there and you have to help her.'

The words came at us from every angle. They were all spoken at once. There were half a dozen layers of sound and information. The terror, the shock, the fear and the urgency was palpable in every voice.

And then there was something else.

'They've got another boy who ran out and raised the alarm. But they've also got a little baby girl. No one's seen the baby.'

Dave and I were already on the move. If it had been possible, we'd have gone up an extra gear after those last, awful words:

'No one's seen the baby.'

The sentence echoed, somehow, on the wind.

'We need to get to the window. Get the short extension ladder.'

The whole team was there to get the job done. There was another crescendo of noise as we got ready. The ladder clattered as we rolled it off the back of the truck. Instructions and confirmations were being shouted across all the vehicles. Dave and I yelled out as we got the ladder across the front lawn and up against the house. There was more noise, like rumbles of thunder, as we extended it to just below the windowsill. That upstairs window would be our new point of entry. I got the nod from John and Dave and headed up there first. Dave was right on my tail. Back at ground level the other team, Charlie and Arfer, had moved from the rear of the property and were now directing water through the open front door. Their aim was to tackle the fire's heart, right through the hall, past the collapsing staircase and into the room at the rear of the house. While I wasn't able to see whether or not they were succeeding, I was first to face the consequences of this new line of attack.

By the time I got towards the top of the ladder, super-heated steam was surging through the whole building. It was swirling up where the stairs had been. It had cut across what was left of the landing. It then followed the path of least resistance to find an escape – which meant it forced its way in a brutal, scalding cloud through the window I was climbing into.

I sensed, then saw, the steam the moment my head got to the top of the ladder. I knew what it could do. I knew naked skin would get poached. Dave, of course, was totally unaware, but I knew he'd have carried on climbing regardless. So that's what I did too. I took my final three steps up the ladder. And I realised, suddenly, how lucky I was. For of all the people on the watch, I'd been asked to test out a variation on our new helmets. I'd been asked to assess it and report on it before a decision was made whether to issue it to us all. The new addition was a sort of neck skirt that was designed to offer extra protection in precisely this sort of situation. It was hard to believe that I could be so lucky. If it worked it would be perfect. So I kept on moving.

I pulled the new skirt thing across and held it tight to my neck and ears. I raised myself another few feet. I dragged the hose-reel along with me. I was ready. I began to aim the water in through the window to start to clear the fire that was aiming to destroy the bedroom. And I felt its power. Fires seem alive, in those first moments that you fight them. They're the enemy. We can't be the ones to blink first. Especially when we've been told there's someone in the midst of it. A mother – and a baby girl.

When the flames had been pushed back far enough by the water, I dived through the open window into the room. Dave was right there behind me, just as I'd have been behind him.

The noise is always intense in a house that is being eaten alive from the inside. Fire on its own can deafen you. When glass is smashing, fixtures and fittings are imploding and floors are collapsing, the aural assault comes from all sides. What I wanted to hear, in those first few seconds in the bedroom, was a mother's voice and a baby's cry. I wanted to hear something, anything, to tell me that both of them were still alive. But there was nothing to hear.

Dave and I began shouting then. We were pushing through the debris as we started our search. We didn't have far to go.

The lady's body was on the floor of the bedroom, right beside where we had both landed. In the horrible pulsing lights of the fire it was clear that she was dead. The flames around her had been ferocious. Her body was in a terrible state. She hadn't just been burned badly. She had been burned right through. I touched her leg. You can't feel anything through our thick gloves. But this lady's leg wouldn't have felt like skin anyhow. It was raw and ragged in some places. It was blackened and blistered in others. These were the worst of times. And they weren't over yet.

With one casualty found, Dave and I moved through the rest of the room, trying to feel for whatever else was there. We always move around the sides, one in each direction. We feel our way, aiming to meet on the far side and then fan out to cover what we might have missed in the middle of the room. We'd not missed anything. There was nothing to find.

There was no sound of the woman's baby. There was no sign of a cot in that room either. At that point there was no way of knowing if that was good or bad news. We had to take it as good. We had to hope that the baby was somewhere else in the house. Somewhere untouched by the fire.

I took another gulp of air as this stage of the task came to an end. We had been fighting the fire in the room throughout the search. We had swamped it with water. We were winning. I directed the hose-reel back at the last licks of fire that were in the room. Then Dave and I moved forward. Unsteady on the floor, we edged out towards the steam-filled landing. We saw the gaping hole where the stairs had been. We focused the water on the flames that were pulsing around the remains of the bedroom doors opposite us. Down below, the other crew were making their own slow but sure progress through this tragic home.

Once the fire had been beaten upstairs, it was time for us to climb down the ladder. Our air supply was dwindling, and we would need fresh cylinders if we were going to be sent back in.

'The mother's there. She's in the bedroom, just where they said she was,' Dave was telling John as we regrouped briefly outside.

'She's dead?'

'Very much so, sir.'

He nodded and turned to the police officer at his side. They then stepped towards the ambulance crew. Dave and I rejoined Nicholas, who handed back our tallies and recorded our return on the board. Very little was said. But a lot was happening.

On the other crew, Charlie and Arfer were still tackling the blaze from below. Slowly, surely and successfully they were moving around the ground floor. By this time we'd been at that property, fighting that fire, for around twenty-five minutes. I felt sweat drip down my back as darkness fell and the smoke and steam started to mix into a horrible, indeterminate grey. I looked at the broken windows of the home, the black stains around every window and door, the gash of damage on the roof. Fire had been – and continued to be – our enemy that night. It had taken hold so fast, and so strongly, that it had taken us this long to control it. It had fought us, just as we had fought it. And it had claimed at least one life.

I snapped out of my thoughts and looked around me. The road outside the house that awful autumn evening was lit by a mass of blue flashing lights. Our appliances, the ambulances and the police cars dominated what had once been a quiet, happy residential road. Until that night. That night it was crammed with neighbours, friends and family members of all ages. People had come from everywhere. More seemed to be arriving all the time. Men, women and children were crying. Some were beyond tears, holding on to each other. Faces were pale. Voices were low.

'Yes, the mother is dead,' I heard John confirm softly to one of the medics as the crowd suddenly surged forward.

'And the baby? Has anyone seen the baby?' The same neighbour who had spoken earlier had got close enough to hear us. There was horror and hysteria in her voice now.

Another equally tense voice spoke up from the crowd before John could get a word in.

'The boys told my wife that she was in a room at the back of the house. It was a downstairs room. She was in her child seat.'

'Where exactly are the boys?' John asked sharply.

'They're with my wife. We know them. They're safe in our house. There's one of the policemen with them too.' It was a man's voice this time. He sounded quiet, authoritative and very, very sad.

The crowd fell back again as Charlie and Arfer stepped away from the side of the house, dragging their hose-reel after them, making sure it was ready, in case it was needed again. They had done all they could for now. I could see the sweat dripping off both men's faces as they put their hands on their hips, sucked in some fresher air and tried to catch their breath. They too handed their tallies to their board operator. They too had little to say.

When the fire had been dealt with, and the investigations had begun, we would be able to paint a fuller picture of what had happened to this tragic family. We had the evidence at the scene and the descriptions from the children and the neighbours. We also had a lifetime of experience from far too many similar, horrible events. This is what we knew.

The mother had been having a lie-down in the front bedroom upstairs. The room where she had died. The neighbours had been right when they had shouted out at us. There had been a baby, a toddler and two older kids in the house with her at the time. The baby and the toddler had been in the downstairs living room, which overlooked the back garden. It was a living room with a gas fire in the grate. It was the room where they hung up laundry to dry.

How many times, how many fires, had we attended that had been caused by clothes hung up to dry? Too many, is the simple answer.

That day the door to the living room had been closed. This had kept the smoke from the fire while the flames took firm hold. It meant no one else knew about the fire till it was too late. At some point, though, the toddler must have run for help. He'd opened the living-room door, left it open behind him, and then run across the hall to the front door. He'd opened it, run through it, and it had slammed behind him as he ran to the house opposite screaming for help.

'Why didn't he run upstairs, to find his mum? Why go to a neighbour?' Nicholas had asked, as we discussed the fire long afterwards.

'It's good that he did,' had been Pete's simple conclusion. 'If he'd gone upstairs, he might not have come down again. That poor little nipper.'

Back at his house on the night in question, a terrible chain of events was underway. Only one window in the house was open, a window on the landing at the top of the stairs. With the downstairs living-room door open, the fire was building its own, very powerful chimney. This had two terrible consequences. The first was that it drew the heat and the smoke upstairs towards the landing window. The second was that it hugely intensified the strength of the fire.

Smoke fills rooms from the top down. That's why it's safest to stay low if you're in a fire. That's why it's better to drag people out along the ground than to swing them up and over our shoulders the way the Hollywood heroes do. And if smoke fills a room from the top down, you can be assured of one thing. It's deadly serious by the time it starts to seep under the gap beneath a bedroom door.

And it was seeping beneath the gap that night. The smoke was indescribably thick by the time the two lads in the up-stairs room were aware of it.

How scared were they when they saw what was coming under their door? Possibly not as scared as they would be a moment later. When they opened the door, they would have been confronted by a wall of thick, moving, malevolent smoke. Piecing together the evidence, it seems the older lads' screams finally woke their mother. She would have opened her bedroom door to discover the same terrifying scene the boys had. But she had got through it. She had got to her eldest kids as the flames started to make their way up the stairs, carving out across the landing and cutting off their escape.

Somehow, through the coughing and the spluttering, the mum had got her boys into the front bedroom. She must have thought the worst was over when she saw her neighbours outside, desperate to help, shouting that the Fire Brigade was on its way and lining up the tallest ladder they could find.

But the boys' mum had made one last, fatal mistake.

She had pulled up the bedroom window to scream for help. But she hadn't closed her bedroom door behind her. Until that moment the smoke had been billowing across the landing and pouring out of the window up there. Now it surged across her room as well. It would have swamped her. House smoke can be acrid, toxic and fatal. It would have suffocated her as she passed first one, then the other of her children down to the arms of her neighbours. We can only assume that the smoke had overcome and defeated her the moment she had done her job.

In the front garden of her shattered home, long before we knew all this for sure, we stood and tried to assess the scene and work out what we could do next. That's when Charlie looked over and saw what had happened to Dave.

'Bloody hell, mate, have you seen your neck?'

He pulled off his helmet and opened his jacket. The skin of his neck, right up to the level of his visor, was red raw. He reached up to touch it with an ungloved hand.

'Your ears, mate – it's got your ears as well,' Charlie said as Dave winced and swore at the pain in his neck. He did the same as his hand touched his scalded ears.

'It was the steam on the way in through the window,' I said. 'I had the new skirt thing on my helmet. It protected me. It did the job.'

'Well, put that in your report,' John said, walking across to us, then turning to Dave. 'Go see the medics. Happen we'll get you to hospital as soon as we're done here,' he said. 'Then you can have the rest of the shift off.'

But we weren't done at the house yet. A call had come from one of the other lads who had gone in to sift through the wreckage of the ground floor. He had found something in the living room. Half-hidden amidst the detritus of burned clothes and so many other objects, he had found something. It was the tiny, blackened hint of the shape of a baby. I'm not sure if we were ever told whether the little girl had died of smoke inhalation or of direct burning. It didn't matter, of course. The poor mite was gone.

It was almost midnight before the house was deemed safe. That was our cue for the next, saddest stage on the journey. It was time for the undertakers to remove the bodies. It was the second time I'd seen those plastic coffins in a matter of weeks.

'Where are the kids? Are they inside? You'll keep them there? We don't want them to see this,' an acutely sensitive John told the older neighbour who was back at his side.

'I'll go to them now. We've tried to put them to bed, but they won't go down. We'll keep them away until you come and tell us,' he said.

The first coffin was for the baby. Sometimes the undertakers bring plastic body bags to scenes like this. Sometimes they bring boxes that are like ordinary coffins, though they're plain and made of plastic. The latter mean more, somehow. They've

got associations that you can't avoid feeling. The body bags
have an official air. They make it clear that an investigation of
some kind will shortly take place. They suggest that removing
the body is part of a wider process. When we're presented with
the boxes – the coffins – it feels different. The bodies inside
will be sent for an autopsy, same as the ones in body bags.
But there's a sense of finality about the boxes. And that night
things were even worse. The box – the coffin – was small. It
was meant for a child and it would hold this baby. It was un-
utterably sad.

I can't imagine how many prayers might have been said as
that short, sad procession went by. But when it had passed,
John looked up. He looked at Dave and I. He gave us a curt
nod. We understood immediately what he meant. It was a
simple and fitting message. Dave and I had found the lady's
body. We would be the ones to help her out of her home this
one, final time.

'I'll carry it up,' I said, holding on to one end of the second
plastic coffin. We placed the short extension ladder in the hole
where the stairs had once been, and gained access to the first-
floor bedroom once more. It was a gruesome task, putting the
body into the coffin, but we did it with as much dignity as we
could. After the lid was secure, we manhandled the box down
our makeshift staircase and out through the front door.

The crowd of neighbours and onlookers fell silent as we
edged this precious cargo past them. Heads bowed and tears
were wiped away as it was carried to the back of the undertakers' van. Those dark-suited, solemn men had taken charge.
I surveyed the scene. Darkness had crept up on us. The shadows were deep and beyond the ugly orange street lights the
night sky seemed endless. Most of the people on the street
waited until the undertaker's van had driven off, then they too

faded away in groups of two or three. The investigators and the police would be in charge of the scene for some time now. Dave was driven off to Casualty to have his burned ears and neck examined. The rest of us packed up our kit, re-stowed everything in the vehicles and headed back to the station in rare silence. It was over.

# 9

# Saying Goodbye

I shaved and showered, ironed my shirt, combed my hair, polished my shoes and got ready to head to the station. But I wasn't heading in for a shift. I was going to a party. And I was miserable as sin.

The party was for Caddie, the old-timer on the watch who had taken me under his wing, acted as my mentor, taught me so much and become my friend. Caddie, who had done it all and seen it all during a lifetime in the brigade. He was retiring, at the grand old age of fifty. We'd always known it was coming, of course. The rest of us had been planning his send-off for months. We had plenty of surprises up our sleeves for him that night. But I'd have done anything to turn the clock back and give him a few more years on Red Watch.

Stanley, one of the grim-faced old-timers from Green Watch, was the first person I saw when I got to the station on the big night.

'It's the end of an era,' I said, the most serious I'd been in ages.

'It's the end of an error, more like!' he joked. The cleverest he'd been since I'd known him. But I didn't laugh.

The bar was so packed that Caddie was hard to spot when I got upstairs. It was testament to how well liked he was that so many people from other watches came along to his send-off

– and that they'd come in so early. Mr and Mrs Thom, the retired couple who used to run the frozen-food shop at the end
of the road and had always come in to give us broken biscuits
and out-of-date food, had driven back into town to see him go.
They'd brought a gift as well. Instead of the usual packaged
food, Mrs Thom had baked something – a big tray of rich,
crispy, lemon-infused Shrewsbury cakes.

'Well, all the best, old man,' I said, forcing my way through
the crowd and passing over a badly wrapped bottle of ginger
wine.

'I'm retiring. I'm not going on a trek across the desert,' he
said. He was in his Sunday best, wearing smart formal trousers, a brown checked shirt and a tie. Everyone else had made
an effort as well. Arfer, who wouldn't have worn a suit to his
own funeral, was the smartest I'd seen him in years. Woody
looked to have ironed his shirt, or at least to have got his wife
to do it for him.

The ladies in our lives – and on this occasion I mean our
work lives, so the cleaners and cook, not our girlfriends and
wives – had made even more of an effort. Maggie was re-
splendent in a red-and-white polka-dot dress the size of a sail.
And she had someone in her wake.

'Mabel!' I exclaimed as I got closer. Mabel, who had been
one of the two cooks to look after us when I first joined the
watch, gave me a typically stern once-over.

'Good to see you've at least taken the time to shave,' she declared after a worrying pause. 'A haircut wouldn't have gone
amiss. But I know you're a busy man.'

'You've certainly not changed,' I told her. 'You're here to
keep order, are you?'

'I'm here to try,' she said firmly. Mabel must have been in
her late seventies by then, but there were few roosts she wasn't

capable of ruling. I'd put my money on her in most situations.

She'd just started to quiz me about my love life and my building work when Charlie pushed past and interrupted. He, of course, wanted to talk about food. Much hilarity ensued as he, Maggie and Mabel competed to dream up the stodgiest food combinations. Across the room, I could see some of our ever-changing roster of agency cleaners in for some free drinks and nibbles. And, of course, a number of our partners and girlfriends. I had my eye on the sister of a friend of mine at the time, a lovely girl called Karen. I'd not got as far as asking her out, at that point. And maybe taking a date to a leaving party like this wasn't a great idea anyway. Because it was already pretty clear that we were going to spend most of the time talking shop – and taking the mickey out of each other.

'Caddie, you're the biggest joker on the watch. What about that time your trousers fell down at the nurses' home?' I heard Pete yell out from the bar as Woody got some music playing on a stereo in the corner. Despite a blast of Level 42 almost drowning out the reply, practically the whole room fell about laughing. I'd not been on the watch back then. But I'd heard the story so often I felt as if I had. And I was more than happy to hear it all again.

'That never happened,' Caddie bellowed.

'It did!' we all shouted back like kids in a chorus. And then we got the cue that we wanted.

'Tell us what happened!' one of the wives shouted. It was our signal to tell the tale yet again.

'It was a night shift,' Pete began. 'It was quiet. We'd all had a skinful. Old George had cooked the dinner.'

'Fish pie. Perfectly burned Cheddar on top of the potato. With greens – cabbage and leek. Both on the watery side.

Badly cooked greens that let the rest of the plate down,' added Charlie.

'Never mind what we ate. It's what we drank that mattered,' said Pete. 'And Caddie drank too much.'

'I never drank too much in my life!' he lied.

'Well, if you weren't the worse for wear, how do you account for the trousers?'

'What about the trousers?' Nicholas shouted above the din.

Pete was shouting too – and furiously signalling Woody to turn Talking Heads down a notch or two. 'Caddie went to bed about 3 a.m. Always was a wuss, our Caddie.'

'It was more like four.'

'It was more like two. You're a lightweight. Always was, always will be. Anyway. To bed it was.'

'Oh God.'

'You're snoring away as usual.'

'Enough!'

'And we got the call at half-past six. Us lot all grab our clobber, hit the pole, get on board the engine and head on out. It's an automatic fire alarm at the nurses' home over at Shrewsbury Hospital. It was full of pretty young ladies. Best place we ever went.' Pete, taking a sharp look from his wife, carried on the story regardless. 'It's not far. But old man Caddie is driving and it takes him a good ten minutes to get us there.'

'That is not true!' shouted an outraged Caddie. I felt his pain. Criticising our driving was the lowest of the low.

'And when we do arrive, what do we find?' asked Pete.

Everyone in the room was paying attention by then. Many of those present didn't know the full story. 'Beautiful women. That's what we find. Half a dozen beautiful women, maybe more. Women in their nightdresses. Women we all want to impress. Women we want to admire us, to look up to us as firemen, and as heroes. And what does our Caddie go and do?'

Everyone looked across at him and he stood up, took a bow and delivered his own punchline.

'I jumped out of the cab, I stood right there in front of everyone. And my blinkin' trousers fell down!'

'He'd burst the top button of his trousers,' Pete explained. 'He was left standing there in nothing but his kegs. Hairy legs, knobbly knees and all. The girls fell about laughing. No wonder I never got a date.'

'Hey, you – we were married by then,' his wife shouted out from her side of the room.

'They were boxer shorts,' added Caddie, inconsequentially. 'Blue ones, with white stripes on them. Rather natty, I thought.'

'And we were back in time for breakfast. Three poached eggs, I had. White toast. Real butter. Just a scraping of Marmite,' said Charlie dreamily.

With that tale told, the old-timers were soon talking about endless other 'good old days' when the bar had been open all hours and the beer had cost next to nothing. Which it still did, as far as I could tell. I watched our two latest cleaners cadge some cigarettes off a cluster of Green Watch guys in the corner. It was clear, even from a distance, that their conversation was more than a little fruity. One of the men was manoeuvring a plastic chair into place. He had a box of matches between his teeth. One of our favourite bar games looked set to begin.

But before it did, I got distracted by another conversation on my side of the room. The talk there was all about our other favourite sport – ice hockey, at which Caddie had unaccountably excelled. 'You're not bad for an old feller,' I'd never hesitated in telling him after each game.

'But how do you play ice hockey around here? Where do

you actually go to play? Do you go to the ice rink in Telford or somewhere?' Dodger's new girlfriend, the rather talkative Cheryl Walton, asked as that strand of the conversation took root.

'Don't be daft! We play right here in the station.'

'How?'

'We make our own ice,' Caddie said with a wink.

'How do you make ice?' she asked.

'By freezing water,' everyone replied, including Dodger – which struck me as a bad move.

'You know what I mean. Where do you play? Tell me or I'm going home,' she said, pretending to sulk. Quite convincing, she was too.

So we told her. We played ice hockey most Saturdays when we were on day shifts. We got the vehicles out of the appliance room. We got the hose-reels out and got the concrete slick and lethal with water and liquid soap. A bar of soap was our puck. Brooms and mops were our sticks.

'We set up goals, we divide into teams and off we go,' said Nicholas, who enjoyed the games as much as I did.

'It's total war. It's pure violence. And Caddie – he plays like a man possessed.'

'I play to win, perhaps.'

'You play to kill. Every week you'd swipe your stick so close to my head you nearly brained me,' said Des.

'Well, 'appen every week you'd done something to deserve it.'

'So there's no actual ice. And you don't have skates. But you still play ice hockey and you nearly kill each other in the process. And you're the ones we rely on to save us when things go wrong. Sometimes I wish I didn't know all this,' Dodger's new girlfriend was saying as Caddie stood up, grabbed an umbrella and nearly took John's head off as he began to demonstrate his goal-scoring prowess.

I looked around as the noise in the room picked up and dozens of different conversations started up. Green Watch and their companions were having a raucous time with a soggy match box. Woody had turned the music back up. Amidst the throng, I could make out the occasional member of White and Blue Watch. The latter were the guys who were actually working that night. They were having as much fun as everyone else, but they'd disappear sharpish if the alert call sounded.

'To Caddie, and to all our friends round the Wrekin,' Pete shouted suddenly. It was a classic local toast and he followed it up by draining the last of his pint and slamming his empty glass on the bar. Ben, manning the pumps for a change, passed over a foaming replacement in the blink of an eye. What a crazy group of guys we all are, I thought.

At the end of the long, late night we all toasted Caddie properly and handed over a card and a present. But in my mind I had toasted him along with Pete. I knew I would miss him more than most. I'd learned more from him than from anyone else. And I hoped that one day I might make half as good a mentor to some other young buck as Caddie had been to me.

# 10

# Carrying the Torch

〜

A sharp and surprisingly cold Welsh wind caught me as I slammed my front door shut and headed down the pavement. Rain was in the air and it felt like the first fingers of autumn were stretching out towards me from the west. Summer was nearly over. A new season was about to begin. I opened my car door fast and jumped inside. Autumn was a busy time for us. There would be barn fires, bonfires and chimney fires – you name it, we'd get it. Drivers would skid and come a cropper on dark, wet nights. All manner of animals would get into trouble out on the farms on the Long Mynd and up on the glorious Shropshire Hills. We'd be worked hard. I'd love every minute, as usual. But I would miss Caddie.

Red Watch wasn't the same without him. John and the various junior officers had always led the watch, but Caddie had been central to it. His approval had mattered to me from my first day in the job. I'd sought it from the very start. I'd learned so much from his slow, steady explanations of what we did and why. I'd always known that some of the stories he told were cleverly designed to prepare me for some of the challenges I'd be facing. He'd been there at my first house fire, and on the day I saw my first dead body – a huge shock for a lanky eighteen-year-old who thought he would live for ever.

He was a steady character and a true pal. Whatever shout

we were on, I'd find myself looking up to see if I'd lived up to his expectations. I still did – till I remembered that he was no longer there.

And was I somehow stepping into his shoes? I felt that one day, out of the blue, as I was working alongside Nicholas on a house fire over in Battlefield, the long since swallowed-up village where, as you might have guessed, the Battle of Shrewsbury took place at the start of the fifteenth century. I can't remember what they were fighting for, to be honest. Nor who won.

The shout itself was one of those bread-and-butter jobs. It was mildly sad, but nothing particularly memorable. A small fire had broken out in an elderly lady's home – a situation we encountered so often that the homes, and indeed the ladies, all seemed to blend into one. They were small, neat, well organised and ever so slightly creaky. They were never flashy and never loud. The women, not the houses, were almost always embarrassed about the fuss. They were almost always upset, though they would struggle to hide the fact.

The birdlike Mrs Donaldson was the perfect example. When we arrived, she was darting around as if she herself was on fire. Somewhere in her early seventies, she was small and pale and sensibly dressed. She was wearing a housecoat, a garment not many people still went in for. It was well worn, but clean. And the lady was in constant motion.

On that particular day Joe and Ben were working as numbers three and four, so they had their breathing apparatus sets on and were first off the engine and into the house. Once again Nicholas was number five, so once again he was in charge of the BA board outside – recording who had gone into the fire and when, so we'd know exactly when their air might run out and when they might need help. Charlie was number two.

Having driven the engine to the scene, he was in charge of the pump that would supply high-pressure water to the hose-reel. He'd then monitor the gauges for the rest of the shout to make sure the flow stayed consistent.

Out in the street, Mrs Donaldson looked from one of us to the other as we got on with our work. She was sensible enough to keep away from the house and the kit. But she was too twitchy to disappear into a neighbour's house for a cup of tea as we'd suggested. She was certainly a nice old bird. If she apologised once for having called us out, she must have apologised a hundred times. If she asked if she could help once, she must have asked two hundred times. And in truth there was absolutely nothing she could do.

The fire had sparked off in her kitchen, which was at the front of the house.

'A tea towel! Of all things, it was a cotton tea towel!' she twittered as the job got underway. 'It was too close to the gas rings. I've never, not in my whole life, done anything that foolish before. I set fire to a tea towel! And me, who's raised three kids, seven grandchildren and does the Christmas lunch every year for the WI.'

'What were you cooking today, my love?' asked Charlie, true to form.

'Egg and chips. I always have egg and chips on a Tuesday,' she said.

Charlie let out a long, low sigh. 'I've not had egg and chips for weeks. Now you've got me all hungry,' he said.

'It's only half-past two. Did you lot not have lunch?' asked the WPC who was waiting around with us. Her name was Jocelyn and she was a scary woman, most of the time. Tall and thin, in her mid-twenties and clearly determined to get on in life.

'Having lunch doesn't stop our Charlie from being hungry,' I told her.

'I would have had enough for two,' Mrs Donaldson said. Then she let out a little cry of alarm and looked past us towards where Joe and Ben were coming out of her front door.

'Don't worry. It'll be all right,' I told her.

She tried to smile, then listened in as they gave their report. It was decent news, thankfully. We'd got there soon enough. 'The tea towel had set the curtains and nets alight,' Joe began.

'They were lace. Lace curtains. I can't abide nets,' she interrupted firmly.

Joe corrected himself. 'It set your curtains and lace curtains alight. It burnt the cupboards either side of them. But after that the fire was all bark and no bite. It probably looked a lot worse than it was.'

And as Mrs Donaldson had shown the good sense to slam the kitchen door shut behind her when she ran to get help, it had been contained in that one small front room.

'The fire is out, ma'am, and the gas and the electrics are all off,' Joe continued. 'You can rest assured that we won't be leaving here until we've checked every inch of your home to make sure that nothing is smouldering away anywhere out of sight. We're ventilating the house now to get rid of what's left of the smoke. My men will go back in to make their final checks in a while. Then we'll do what we can to help you with the damage.'

'Is the kitchen ruined?'

'It's not going to look good. We'll have to pull some of your woodwork and cupboards apart when we check for embers. But as long as we don't get called out on another job, we're more than happy to help pull any damaged cabinets outside so you can dispose of them properly.'

'You don't need to do that,' she began.

'We don't need to, but we'd like to.'

Joe and Ben got to work, probably looking like blue-suited giants in the lady's tiny, ship's galley of a kitchen, while we wound the hose-reels back onto their drums and re-stowed the rest of the kit.

'With the kitchen gone, I can't even offer you a cup of tea. All your work and I can't even do that. I'll just go and ... I'll just go and ...' she said, tailing off again, unsure of what exactly she might go and do. Suddenly she looked on the point of tears. It was as if the reality of what had happened had finally hit her – and hit her hard. She seemed smaller than ever in that moment, and very old.

'Why don't you show me your garden, love?' Jocelyn asked, before turning quickly to the other Joe for his approval. 'It's safe to go to the back of the house, isn't it?'

'Be my guest.'

The pair of them disappeared through the back gate. We stayed on and talked to a couple of neighbours who'd come by to see what all the fuss was about, but once they'd gone there wasn't much for the rest of us to do. After a while Nicholas and I walked round the side of the house, intrigued to see how the tour of the garden could possibly be taking so long.

When we got through the gate we saw Jocelyn, on her own, standing by the French windows to the back lounge. 'She wanted to go in there. I told her it was OK as long as she stayed in the living room.'

We took a look and then stepped inside. It was a neat, comfortable and entirely grandmotherly room. There were some straight-backed armchairs, a set of side tables, a small telly and a big, dark wooden dresser. Every inch of every shelf was covered in china figurines. And Mrs Donaldson was standing in front of it. She was wearing yellow washing-up gloves and had a bright orange duster in her hand.

'Got to keep these clean,' she said when she saw us approach. 'They get dusty every day. I've never known such dust as we get around here. I grew up in Cumberland, you know. We only got half the dust out there. Living here, you need to keep on top of dust every single day,' she said. There was an odd intensity in her manner, and more than a hint of tears in her watery blue eyes.

Nicholas stepped forward. There was a worried frown on his face. I sensed that he was about to swoop on her and usher her back outside. 'Mrs Donaldson, you really don't need to do this now,' he began.

I stepped forward myself. 'It takes a while to clean each of these, doesn't it?' I said, picking up a pale-coloured and very delicate ballet dancer. 'My mum collects those little dogs and the little china houses. Dust gets everywhere on those. Too many corners to clean on the little houses.'

'Indeed there are,' the lady said, grasping at my interest the way a drowning man grasps at a plank of wood. 'Look at this one,' she said, taking the ballet dancer from me. 'It captures the dust like nobody's business. Now it's got your dirty, sooty fingerprints on it as well, you naughty young man. That's even more for me to do. The job never ends, I tell you. So, if you two gentlemen will leave me to it, I'll get on much faster on my own.'

'We'll call you if we need you,' I said – and led a still-frowning Nicholas out of the room. 'It's shock,' I told him when we were out of earshot in the garden. 'Everyone reacts differently. It's part of our job to spot it. Provided it's not dangerous, we let people get on with it. Cleaning is obviously what this lady does best. She's on edge, but it's helping her get through this and it's not harming anyone. She's safe. She's not exactly happy, but she's OK. We need to leave her be. There's no point in stopping her.'

Nicholas nodded slowly and gave a rueful smile. Lesson learned, he seemed to be saying. And I smiled. It was Caddie and me, all those years ago. Only this time I was the experienced fireman passing on knowledge to a new recruit. This was such a simple, basic and very human lesson. But I hope Caddie would have approved.

# 11

# That Doggy in the Window

The fire had been burning for some time – and it would continue to do so for some time yet. No one seemed too bothered by its cause. 'They do say these things 'appen – and they do always seem to 'appen to me,' seemed to be the farmer's view of the matter. He introduced himself as Dale Jinman. He seemed tired and haggard behind his weather-beaten tan. He had a boxer's broken nose, dark, deep-set eyes and an overwhelming air of proud exhaustion.

We were at a smart-looking farm slap bang in the middle of nowhere. The farmer had reported a fire in an old machinery shed on his main yard. It had all manner of junk and combustible materials in it, we were told, the way most farm barns did. But it also had a huge amount of straw inside. The usual big, heavy bales were stacked one on top of the other and half a dozen deep. The barn had a metal girder frame with wooden cladding on top of the eight-foot sleepers that formed the sides and back wall. Next to it on one side was a brick-built cowshed. A similar but slightly smaller building full of cow pens was to the other side. The farmhouse itself was a few steps away, lost behind a thick mass of ivy, at the far end of the yard.

When our appliances arrived it was only the barn in the middle that was ablaze. But the winds that autumn day were strong and changeable. They fanned the flames one moment, then let the flames burn down a little the next, then they moved everything in a different direction straight afterwards. The farmer, sensing the danger, had called us to make sure the situation didn't get any worse. Losing the contents of the barn was bad enough. He certainly didn't want to lose its structure as well – or any of his neighbouring buildings.

We were happy to help him. The Fire Brigade has more rules that I care to count, but 'Don't get called back' is one of the most important. You don't ever want to leave the scene of a fire without being sure the danger has passed. You don't want hidden embers to catch the minute your back is turned. But there's another, equally important, rule: 'Don't let a fire spread'. You must try to contain everything. Wind is only one of your enemies there.

'Right, Windsor, get some water on the front of the barn. Dodger, you and Simon start to damp down the cowshed. You lot tackle the other building,' John instructed as we all jumped down onto the dry dirt of the yard.

We had two appliances on the site and got all the respective jets of water going fast, dousing the fire-facing sides of both brick buildings to help stop the fire from jumping. The farm-house was upwind and looked to be far enough away from danger. But we all knew that could change fast. So we wanted our initial firebreaks to be in place as soon as possible.

What we didn't really tackle was the blaze itself. We could have given it a go, if required. We would certainly jump in if it looked set to do some real damage, or if the barn's struc-ture was in danger. But bales of straw are tougher than they look. They work like a thatched roof. Water only penetrates an inch or so into the bale while the rest of it burns away mer-rily. Anyway, putting the fire out wouldn't help this farmer. The barn was where he stored his feeding straw and it was worthless now. Animals refuse to eat straw once it has been contaminated by even a whiff of smoke.

The other reason we stood back and watched the blaze was equally practical. Farmers are OK about getting a pile of moderately useful ash to play with after a barn fire. They're not so keen on being left to move a vast and unwieldy pile of half-burned, newly water-sodden and utterly worthless bales of straw. So our task that day was to provide our tired farmer with that big pile of moderately useful ash. Once the firebreak was up and all the danger had passed, we would be on a watching brief for the rest of the shout.

Everything felt calm and controlled as the water made its icy arc towards the other buildings and splashed all over them. It was late afternoon and the sky was wide, clear and made up of the palest of blues. The colours seemed to be piled up on each other, an ever deeper set of shades and tones. There was something peaceful and timeless to it. I loved being so far out in the country. I liked the sense of freedom you get. I could understand why the farmers enjoyed their glorious isolation. And, of course, I liked the fact that we stood a fair chance of getting some tea and maybe some lovely home-made grub from the farmer's wife as the waiting game got underway. It was incredible, sometimes, the food we were offered in the far reaches of the county. Farming families ate incredibly well. Charlie wasn't on either of our appliances that day. I was looking forward to winding him up over what he'd missed.

Lost in my daydream, and feeling my stomach start to rumble, I didn't hear the two young children running up behind me. But I woke up fast. They seemed to have come out of nowhere. They were alongside me in a flash and got past me in an instant. And in some bizarre moment of madness they were making for the door of the burning barn.

'Oi! You two! Stop! Get back. Get away from there!' I yelled.

The pair stopped stock-still. They were within twelve feet of the barn. They hesitated, but only for a second. I could tell from the way they were standing that they were about to move forward again. Something was drawing them into danger. And whatever it was, I had to sort it out.

'Stay exactly where you are!' I yelled, louder this time. I sensed the pair waver. I saw them look at each other. Then I saw their heads fall in defeat. I ran forward, scooping them up and pushing them back and away from the fire. Two dirty, pinched and panicking faces looked at me as I released them a safe distance away in the yard. The elder of the two, a girl called Olivia, was probably about ten, the other, a boy called Dan was a couple of years younger. I assumed they were the farmer's children. Both were wearing faded jeans and thick check shirts, like their dad. It was clear they were two deeply worried children desperately trying to look strong and not to cry. But why? And what was in the barn?

'Sir, it's our dog. Our dog is in there, sir,' Olivia said, jabbing a finger towards the burning barn. Sympathy and understanding hit me as one.

'He sleeps there, sir. He's not been well. He's a sheepdog and he's old. We're just home from school and we don't know where he is, sir,' said Dan. He could barely breathe he was so upset. He looked as if he was going to run straight back to the burning barn and try to force his way in.

'We're doing our best to stop this blaze from spreading. We've not seen your dog, but if he was inside the barn then he'll have got out long before now. He'll have taken to the hills. You can be sure he's watching all this from somewhere safe. You should be too. Where's your dad gone?'

The kids looked around them. 'Dad's talking to your boss on the other side of the cowshed,' Olivia said.

I was on my own with the pair of them in the middle of the yard.

'What kind of dog is it?' I asked, feeling sorry for the kids, trying to calm them down and keep them with me.

'He's a border collie.'

'His name's Bosun.'

'He's old. I wanted him to live in the house with us, but Mum said no.'

'He's always slept in the barn. But he's hurt his leg. He got an infection.'

'I wanted to sleep in the barn with him till it got better, but Mum said no to that as well.'

I sighed. Farm kids don't normally get sentimental about their animals. Bosun must have been special. He must still be special, I thought, changing the tense. For there was no reason to think he was still in the barn – was there?

'When did you last see him?' I asked, trying to sound as casual as possible.

The kids looked at each other. 'First thing before school. But Mum said they've not seen him since Dad spotted the fire. They should have told us sooner. No one's seen him all the time you've been here.' The young lad looked up at me again. 'I can get a picture of him, if you want.'

'It's OK, son,' I said. 'He'll be here somewhere.' We stayed silent for a few moments. And then I couldn't help myself. 'Is Bosun normally tied up, when he's in the barn?' I asked, not really wanting to hear the answer.

The two of them lowered their heads and didn't reply. I could see Olivia clench and unclench her fists. She was sway-ing on her feet, looking as if she might lurch towards the barn.

Her brother meanwhile had squeezed his eyes tight. Tears were trickling out. It could have been the smoke. But it wasn't. The message was clear. Their dog had been tied up.

'Look, there's nothing we can do from here except watch the fire and let it burn itself out. That's what all of us are doing now. We calm it down on the edges then check the way the winds blow. Stand behind me. Drag this hose-reel a bit to the left, so it doesn't loop out so widely. You can help in loads of ways. The sooner we get things sorted here, the sooner we can get inside the barn and check that Bosun's not there and everything is OK. And it will be OK, I'm sure of it.'

I got the pair working with me for a while. I found them jobs they could do. They were unnecessary things. Distractions. And all the while I kept hoping that Bosun might come loping or limping around the corner to see what all the fuss was about. I'd told the kids he had almost certainly taken to the hills, but I didn't believe it. And neither did they.

'Olivia, Dan, come back here now!' A woman I took to be the children's mum had come into our part of the yard. She was tall, slim and had straw-blonde hair tied up in some sort of sexy, possibly Scandinavian twist. She was wearing jeans and yet another checked shirt, this time in shades of pale, faded green. The whole family seemed to wear the same clothes, I thought. That had to mean they were close, right? It had to mean the kids would be looked after if bad news came.

'Go see your mum,' I said, giving them a push. I smiled a greeting at her and got a quick, tired smile in reply. Behind her I could see John and Woody starting off on a walk-around. That probably meant we were bang on target with the firebreak. The fire itself was still burning hard in the main barn. Farm fires tend to give off a lot of smoke – from the straw and all the random kit that lies around and gets caught up in them. This one was no exception. It was billowing out of the few openings. On a clear, crisp day like this you'd be able to see it for miles around.

I stepped towards John to ask for an update. In the corner of my eye I saw the two kids shuffle, and then run, towards their mum. They stood in front of her, both talking on top of each other. They started to shout and pointed towards the barn, to the fire. She stepped back. She shook her head angrily. She took a swipe at the young boy. She slapped him round the head. Then she pulled him close. She pulled Olivia close as well. She leaned in and down on them, wrapping her arms around them for a moment as if she'd never let go.

'We're getting there, wind's not moved and the worst's over. Just a case of watching over it and be ready for the unexpected,' said John, understandably relaxed about it all.

'You've not seen a dog? A border collie? An old one?' I asked, hoping my voice wouldn't carry.

'Yon farmer said the dog was inside the barn,' John said, equally softly.

'Was he tied up?'

John looked grim. 'Worse than that. He was chained.'

John, Woody and the farmer carried on with their walk-round. The fire was as intense as ever and generating a lot of heat. When there's nothing else to worry about, fires like this can be strangely enjoyable to watch. Seeing tall piles of straw eat themselves up, fold in on each other and slowly disappear can be mesmerising. It can be beautiful too. There are more colours in a fire than most people realise. There's a rhythm to them as well. 'They burn like a ballet,' someone on the watch once said, years ago, in an uncharacteristically poetic mood.

The flames certainly danced. But something told me I wasn't going to feel any of the usual satisfaction today. I kept thinking about those kids' grubby, desperate faces. I thought about the woman who'd taken a swing at them for something they'd said. Then held them close.

Less than ten minutes later the flames were still ripping through their supply of fuel. The farmer's wife had come back out, carrying a tray full of mugs of tea.

'My children are going spare,' she told us. We all knew what she meant.

'We can take a look in a while, but there's not much chance. It's silent in there. Silent as the grave,' said Dodger. Not the best man at choosing the right thing to say, our Dodger.

The kids' mum, grateful all the same, wandered back to her home on the other side of the yard, which was all mud, straw, soot and oil-stained puddles. And then, a few minutes later, when it was only us men in the farmyard, we found him. He had somehow managed to get out of the barn itself. But he'd not got far.

'He was underneath it at the back. God knows why he was there. Looks like he'd slipped his collar and was trying to dig a hole to get away. I saw him, suddenly, through the smoke,' said Woody. 'I saw the patch of white on his back.'

'Why didn't he just run away?' John mused. 'Daft feller,' he said, looking down at something we hoped the kids from the farm would never see.

Parts of Bosun's front legs had been burned. The fur and the flesh had gone. Bone showed through. On his rump a broad patch of fur had been burned away too. His skin there was badly flayed. Woody had run to the barn and dragged Bosun out by his hind legs. The dog was now covered in mud and dirt and soot. His head and face were filthy. His tongue was lolling out of the side of his mouth. One eye was open. The other was cut and caked with dirt.

'The poor thing. What a way to go,' Woody repeated softly.

Instinctively, we looked across the yard. The farmhouse door was on the far side of the yard, to the west. We seemed to be well shielded from most of the windows. No one was coming. At least not then.

'What are we going to do with him?' Dodger asked. 'And who's going to tell the kids?'

There was a long, difficult silence. Lots of the guys on the watch had kids themselves. And jokes apart, we all had hearts.

'Put him on the fire,' John said in the end.

'What?'

'Put him on the fire. They won't want to see him like this. We can't hide him. There's nowhere else for him to go. Put him on the fire and that can be the end to it.'

'You're sure?'

John sighed again. 'What good would there be in letting those kids see what happened? Look at him. Their dog did not die a good or an easy death. Do we want them to know that? Look at his left eye. Look at the bones sticking through his legs. Do we want them to remember him like this? I say that we don't.'

'What if they find his bones?'

'There'll be no bones. Not if we do it now while the heat is still on. We can tell their dad, anyhow. He can be ready to hide anything that's left.' There was silence. 'So what do we say?' John asked.

I looked him in the eye. It was clear that this was one of those rare moments when normal rules don't apply. The Fire Brigade, back then at least, was not about consensus or committee decisions. It was about good old-fashioned hierarchies.

The service still had deep military roots. It was about command structures. It was about one man at the top making a decision everyone else followed to the letter. In ordinary, operational situations that one man never, ever asked what the rest of us might think. But deciding what to do about two heartbroken little kids was not an ordinary, operational situation. John was right to ask us our thoughts. We were right to all take the same line.

'We should put him on the fire,' we said, as one.

And that, unfortunately, was when it all went wrong.

The barn in front of us had a loophole in the gable end, about fifteen or twenty feet up in the air. Bales of hay or straw get pitched through there as the store fills up. The flames had nibbled away at parts of the structure. But the sides, and the main wall in front of us, were still very much intact. On the other side of this wall was where the flames had been the strongest and the embers were the hottest. That was where Bosun had to go, if he was to disappear forever.

'You want me to throw him through the loophole?'

'It's the only way to get him in there.'

'It's a long way up.'

'It's no more than twenty feet.'

'It's not going to be very dignified. None of them can see from the windows? The kids aren't out? No one's coming?' Woody asked.

'It's all clear. Do it now.'

He did. But he didn't do it well. He lobbed the old sheepdog's body up high. Woody had always been one of the best players on our volleyball team. Over the past few weeks we'd had some quiet mornings so we'd had more games than usual. They'd been faster and wilder than normal as well. We had slammed the ball around ferociously. I did well, because I was so tall and because I was young. But Woody did well because he was strong. He was one of the lads who'd taken up some of Robin's body-building techniques. He'd brought some new dumb-bells to add to the ones in the storeroom. He bragged about the weights he lifted in the leisure centre he'd joined in town. And he loved making sure the girls could see his biceps when we were having a few sneaky drinks down the pub. But the muscles, and all the training, let him down badly that day in the farmyard.

'Do it now,' John repeated.

Woody gave him a last, anguished look. Then he made the throw. Bosun's lifeless body rose from his arms. Woody had aimed right at the opening. Everything seemed to do that slow-motion thing you see in films. Bosun's body twisted in the air. It got right up to the gap. It was perfectly in line. Ultimately this was all about getting the aim, the trajectory and the timing right. It was like Daley Thompson doing the pole vault or the high jump at the Olympics. But pole vaulters and high jumpers sometimes ruin everything by touching the bar. Poor, dead Bosun touched his equivalent of the bar that day. He landed, with a soft thump, on the edge of the opening. His body seemed to rest there on the frame. It swayed for a moment as it settled. It looked as if it might topple forward into the flames. Or back into the yard.

But it did neither. It wobbled one more time. Then it went still. Bosun was perched, face forward, on the wooden sill of the loophole, halfway in and halfway out of the barn. His rump, his two hind legs and his badly burned tail were sticking out. And there was something more. His tail seemed to move – to wag – when it was caught by a sudden gust of wind.

'Bugger,' said Woody.

'Oh crap,' said John.

And the rest of us said something even worse.

'What the effing hell do we do now?' Woody asked, panic in his voice. 'We can't let the kids see this.'

'It's disrespectful,' said Dodger unhelpfully. Woody looked as if he might go for him. Funny that this situation somehow meant so much to all of us.

'Woody, you'll get a pole or a ladder and you'll do it right now,' said John in full hierarchical command mode again. 'Windsor, keep watch. Do not under any account allow that family into the yard.'

As if! I got in position and prepared to repel all boarders. Woody and the others brought both pole and ladder. He positioned the former against the side of the burning barn. It was a ridiculously risky thing to do. I can't imagine that anyone would do it today, more's the pity. But Woody got ready to do it then. He got ready to climb up and give Bosun the push he needed. But at that exact moment the farmhouse kitchen door was flung open. And the children came tumbling out.

I ran towards them. 'Hey, hold on, stay there! Stop! It's dangerous!' There was real, genuine panic in my voice. It came across. They both froze, the way they had frozen the first time I'd yelled at them. I carried on running. 'Do not move!' Their mum was at the kitchen door now. And their dad, the farmer. 'Stay there, all of you, stay there!' The panic in my voice was something we never, ever allow people to hear when there's a fire or a genuine emergency. But a dead dog? I was happy to broadcast fear on all frequencies as long as it gave Woody enough time to get up that blinkin' ladder or grab a broomstick and push Bosun out of sight for good.

'What's up? Is it the barn? Is it going to collapse? Has the fire spread? I thought you said it was under control? I'm not having anything happen to my cowsheds or my pens. What the hell is going on?' The farmer fired out the questions fast. He was worried and he was angry. He was determined too. He saw no reason to follow anyone else's orders in his own farmyard. I'd have to grab him to stop him. Did a dead dog warrant that?

'The fire is under control,' I began vaguely, unsure of what I might say next.

'And everything is going to be fine,' said John, arriving at my side. 'A slight misunderstanding. You are more than welcome to look,' he said, his smile a little too wide, trying too hard to look natural. I flashed him a glance as we stood there. He gave the smallest of nods.

'Stay close to me,' the kids' mum said to them as we proceeded across the muddy yard to look at the barn. I had a feeling she knew something was up. I looked to my boots and tried not to meet her eyes.

'We've been checking the structure one last time. Everything is going to be fine,' John repeated. Woody and Dodger passed us on the way back to the engine with the ladder. A broomstick lay on the ground ahead of us. I said a silent thank you in my head. Then I allowed my glance to travel across the roadway, towards the barn, up its back wall and across to the gap in the gable end. Would I see the hindquarters of poor Bosun perched up there, looking for all the world like a dog at play? I didn't. The front of the barn looked exactly the way it should have. My very real, very rare panic was over.

We stayed at that farm for at least another hour. I walked round the yard, and into a nearby field for a better view of what was going on. John took the two kids for a quick tour of the appliances. We let them sit in the driver's seat. Arfer, who normally hated kids, even let them set off the siren. We did all we could to distract them. None of us said what had happened. Neither did we lie to them.

'Wherever he is now, he was lucky to have you as his owners. He won't forget you,' I said as we got ready to leave.

Then I made the mistake of meeting their eyes. They knew. It was totally clear that they knew. Farm kids do.

'Thank you, sir,' Olivia said. Her brother just stood there looking lost.

## 12

# Whiskers on the Carpet

'You think they'll ever find the body?' Woody asked in the cab as we bounced over the rutted country roads and round the sharp corners of all those farm lanes.

'They might smell him. It'll be like the summer barbeque at the White Hart,' said Dodger. 'Flat warm beer and dog burgers!' And then, at long last, we did what firemen and all emergency services staff always do. We started to laugh. We laughed so much it hurt. We weren't being cruel – everything we'd just done had been an attempt to be kind. But looking back it had been like some surreal black comedy. And the tension had been so high it was a massive relief to let it break.

'I have never, ever seen anything so funny. That poor effing dog. Suspended halfway up a barn wall. Like some sort of ornament. A nodding dog. Wagging its bleedin' tail at us.'

'And what kind of throw was that, Woody? What kind of girl's blouse of a throw? You are out of the volleyball team for good.'

'It was like everything went black. It was the shape of him. His weight was all over the place. It wasn't like throwing a ball or a rope. It was like throwing a dead body.'

'It *was* throwing a dead body, you blitherin' idiot. But that was the point. You should have been ready.'

'Well, you do it next time.'

'There's never going to be a next time.'

'And when those kids came out of the kitchen door? I thought I was going to have a heart attack.'

'Woody was up that ladder like a rat up a drainpipe. He was in it to win it. He's not moved so fast since the beer tent went half-price at last summer's beer festival.'

'And don't forget I had to put up with that dog's wagging, blasted tail in my face when I got up there! That damn tail was wagging in the wind. I thought he'd come alive and was going to bite my arm off!' Woody rounded the conversation out as we creased up laughing again.

We calmed down a tad as the appliance crashed over yet another cattle grate and swung through half a dozen stone buildings in a hamlet that did at least offer an attractive-looking country pub. If I ever decide to ask her out, it will be a nice place to come back to with Karen in the summer, I thought, looking at the wooden benches and tables on a lawn that slipped down towards a stream. Most of us were lost in our own thoughts for a while. And then, as something new occurred to Woody up front, he got us started all over again.

'It was like the cat – that damn cat over in Belle Vue. It was like that, all over again!'

'What cat?' asked Dodger.

'The dead one, of course.'

Dodger still looked blank. 'You'll have to narrow it down a bit more, old man. The one that got run over by the fire engine after they'd just rescued it? That's an urban myth, that is.'

'No, you idiot, the one in that fierce old woman's house in Belle Vue.'

'You're going to have to remind me,' Dodger said.

I relaxed, smiled and settled back in my seat. I had a pretty good idea what the story was. If I was right, I was more than happy to hear it again. We had half an hour to go before we got back to base. Long drives through the glorious Shropshire countryside were perfect for our tall tales and smoky stories. Especially silly ones like this.

'It was a little old lady who'd been drying her not-so-smalls in front of an electric fire,' Woody began. As if that narrowed things down. We had that scenario all the time. 'A lot of polyester in those smalls. That's why there was so much smoke. She wasn't on the phone, but a neighbour called so we got there fast. It was mid-morning, if memory serves me well.'

'It was early afternoon. We'd had liver and bacon for lunch. Sprouts and peas on the side. Fresh peas, not frozen. Tinned peaches and crumble for afters. With hot custard made from scratch, not out of a tin or a packet. Martin and Simon had done us proud for a change,' offered Charlie.

'Charlie, that's got sod all to do with it, so keep quiet if you can,' said Woody. 'It was in Belle Vue, just past the Old Bear pub or whatever it's called. It was a bungalow. Quite a new one. Well maintained. Not like the jerry-built jobs you do, Windsor.'

I let that one go by. But Charlie couldn't, in fact, keep quiet.

'Hold on a moment. It wasn't her smalls in front of the fire that set this one off. It was a chip-pan fire in the kitchen. Or possibly a frying pan,' interrupted Charlie.

'Trust you to remember that.'

'But it was. That's why the smoke was so thick. Not the nylon in her smalls.'

Woody nodded and actually gave a shrug of agreement. 'Charlie, I think you're right, as it happens. It was the kitchen where it started. And it was indeed a chip pan. The smoke was acrid as anything.'

'We soon got it contained. Nice kitchen, lots of surfaces to work on. Or at least, there had been,' said Charlie.

'Nice lady as well,' said Woody. 'Little bit reserved and proper, but very bothered about disturbing us. Never had to call the Fire Brigade before in her life. Never troubled anyone. She was mortified, grateful, apologetic as you like. Nice old biddy. Or so we thought at first.'

'And what about her pussy?' Dodger asked.

The five of us laughed so hard we nearly swerved off the road.

'The dear lady's cat was missing,' Woody pronounced when order had been restored. 'She was most concerned. She was actually very upset, and so were we. She said the cat always slept in front of the fire in the living room. She said he, or she, was hard of hearing and slightly blind. She might not have known about the fire until it was too late.'

'When the fire was out, which was almost straight away, we set to with the clear-up,' began Charlie, happy to take up the story. Clear-ups are part of our job. We're there to put out fires, to effect rescues, save lives and sort out any other assorted emergencies. Then it's our responsibility to help with what's known as salvage, or clearing up the mess created by the fire – and by us putting the fire out. If an old lady, living alone, needs a hand putting her home back together then we'd offer it.

'The smoke had spread through to the living room. And the damage in this room was really bad. We reckoned the cat must have been trapped there and it had gone crazy. It had done the wall of death, circling round the room, knocking all her precious china off its shelves and smashing all her photo frames. Then it had conked out and died, right there in the middle of the floor.'

'The woman herself had gone next door to help her neighbour make us all a pot of tea,' said Woody.

'Cheap, supermarket biscuits,' added Charlie, with a sad shake of the head.

'We were in the living room, pulling out the wrecked furniture. The sun was shining in through the bay window out front. The whole room was covered in black dust.' I could picture it. When smoke like that builds up, the heavier particles sink, almost like black snow, and cover every surface. 'That was when I saw it. A lump on the floor, right in the middle of the room. A cat-shaped lump.'

'We decided it was too cruel to tell her or show it to her,' he continued. 'She was a nice old dear. It was better to tell her that her beloved moggie must have escaped and was living a better life with a not-so-near neighbour. It was the kindest thing to do.'

'So what did you do?'

'I picked the cat up off the floor. I was going to put it in a bag and we'd dispose of it when we got back the station. I carried the body out to the engine. The lady was still in next-door's kitchen—'

'Custard creams. Or were they bourbons?' mused Charlie, as if it mattered.

'The lady was still in her neighbour's kitchen and didn't see a thing. I got the body stashed away and came back into her lounge for a final check on the job. That's when I saw it. You couldn't actually miss it. The cat had died on the floor, a heart attack, probably. It had stayed there, stretched out in death as it had been in life. The fire had done its thing all around. The smoke, thick and acrid as anything, had left its mark on every inch of the carpet – and on every inch of the cat.'

'So? I don't understand what the problem was,' said Nicholas, pitching in from the rear seat for the first time since the story had begun.

'Think about it, lad,' Woody said. 'When the cat was no longer in situ there was a crystal-clear, entirely sharp reverse outline of its body on the carpet. The whole of the carpet was jet black where the smoke had settled. The place where the cat had been was ice-cream coloured, almost white.'

'It was like the reverse of one of those chalk outlines they put round dead bodies in America. It was the perfect outline of a cat. You couldn't miss it. I swear you could even see its whiskers.'

'What did you do? Scuff it about?'

'That's what you'd think, isn't it? But funnily enough, and I don't quite recall why, that's not what we did. Maybe there wasn't enough to scuff. I think, perhaps, we'd done too good a job on the clear-up by that point. There was no debris left to use.'

'So what did you do?'

'We went outside to where the woman emptied the ash from her coal fire. We took a spade. We dug out a patch of ash. We carried it into the house. We walked down the hall with it. And that's when the dear old lady came in the back door with her tray of tea and biscuits.'

'Bourbons,' said Charlie decisively.

'What did she say?'

'She let rip, if I remember rightly. It was probably the stress of it all. But she forgot her manners altogether. She was furious. She'd been as meek and mild as anything till that moment. Then she went off like a rocket. 'What the bloody hell are you doing bringing all that dirt into my house?' was how she began.

'And?'

'And the gaffer was tongue-tied. He was this high, all of a sudden,' said Woody, making a sign about an inch high with his fingers.

'I was,' John admitted with a rueful smile. 'I sort of stood there, halfway down her hall, holding a spade full of ash.'

'Did she hit you?'

John gave a loud guffaw. 'Steady on, lad. We didn't quite come to blows. I just took a deep breath and told her it was all part of our training. I said it was a vital fire prevention measure to return some of the debris of a fire to the room where it had started, a set amount of time after the last of the flames had gone out. I told her to wait outside the living room for one moment while we carried out this sensitive procedure. Then I took in the pile of ash, covered up the outline of her dear departed moggy and let the good lady in. She'd got her manners back and I swear she never suspected a thing.'

# 13

# Back to School

∞

How old do you have to be before you stop feeling like a naughty schoolboy when you're called to your boss's office? Fifty, I reckon. Or maybe sixty. Either way, that was how I felt at twenty-seven when I was told that John wanted to see me downstairs.

I'd been up in the bar feeling bored, to be honest. We were back on nights. We'd done a drill, got into our overalls and were waiting for Des and Martin to give the call that dinner was on the hatch. There wasn't much on the telly, I'd read the papers and didn't feel like listening in as Arfer told one of his madly exaggerated stories about how many cabinets and kitchen dressers he'd carried singlehandedly out of some fourth-floor flat at the weekend.

'Hello, you wanted to see me?'

I'd come down the stairs, not the pole. I stood on the threshold of John's den. I really did feel as if I was back at school, waiting to see the headmaster about the state of my uniform or some rule I'd broken.

John had a useful little office on the ground floor of the station. One of the station's two phones was in there, the other being in the watch room next door where the first calls came in when there was a shout. He had a row of big metal filing cabinets, some of which were used for station business, though most of them were stuffed with details of all his building jobs and contracts. A mess of other unusual and unlikely kit was in the corner. I could see a fishing rod, a pair of old tennis shoes, a camping stove and a spare gas canister and one or two pictures with broken glass in their frames.

That evening John was sitting back in his chair, smoke swirling pleasantly round his head. The chair had those little wheels on it and went up and down. Sometimes Nicholas and I played dodgems on it when we hoped no one was looking. The shoulder-sized dent in the nearest filing cabinet had been one of ours.

John stubbed out his cigarette and picked up a couple of pages of typewritten paper. 'You've got a head for heights, haven't you, Windsor?' he asked. I relaxed straight away. If he was using my old nickname – from my surname, I've heard it forever – then I couldn't be in too much trouble.

I had a sudden flashback to the first job I'd applied for at eighteen. I'd had a real desire to join the RAF as a helicopter pilot, and had turned up to a sort of induction or assessment day at Biggin Hill, Kent. There'd been more than eighty of us hoping to get one of only three places in the next round of selections. I'd not been one of the lucky three. Back home, I'd kept my head high – quite literally. I'd applied for a job as a steeplejack. That assessment day was in the form of a height test, which required me to climb up sixteen vertical ladders on the side of a three-hundred-foot chimney. I'd done it without a wobble – or any kind of safety harness for that matter. I got offered the job – but turned it down when I realised it only paid £27 a week. Straight after that I'd heard a pal talk about the Fire Brigade so I applied for that instead. Best decision I ever made.

'I don't mind heights,' I acknowledged to John, thinking back to the view from the top of that three-hundred-foot tower. 'I still go climbing sometimes on my time off. I go hang-gliding off the Long Mynd. I'm even thinking of learning to fly a microlight over at Longmarston Airfield, as it happens. The views around that neck of the woods are supposed to be incredible.'

'Well, I'm sure they are. Whatever a microlight might be.' John tapped the pieces of paper he'd put on his desk. 'I've got something here that might interest you.' He pushed them towards me. I read fast and skimmed over a few sections. But I couldn't stop myself from smiling when I got to the end. It seemed that the Fire Service was beefing up its cliff rescue capabilities. The bosses wanted to kick off by training up one person from each watch. This man would then take charge on any relevant shouts and help train up the rest of his watch through all the usual drills. The training was going to be done at a residential centre over in Wales – and it was due to start in three weeks' time.

'It sounds fantastic, exactly the kind of thing I like,' I said in a rush. 'Are you offering it to me?'

'Is there anyone else in the room with you?'

'Then I'd love it. I'd be over the moon.'

Because I'd got into rock climbing with my old mate Tommy I reckoned I might have a head-start on the rest of the watch. I knew knots, ropes, climbing kit. I also knew that this kind of thing was long overdue. The course would cover going up – for things like cliff rescues. It would also cover going down – so we could help people trapped in mines and caves. Rural Shropshire certainly had more than its fair share of the latter two. We had disused, forgotten tin and lead mines all over. We had caves all around the place too. And we had plenty of cliffs to boot. At the moment we tackled any jobs that came up in such places with the two most important pieces of Fire Brigade equipment – flexibility and good old-fashioned imagination. 'We've only got a limited number of tools for an unlimited number of situations,' Caddie had told me, back when I'd started out on the watch nearly seven years ago. 'Experience is the one thing you can't buy in a shop,' had been one of his other favourite phrases. But you can learn things. And I knew the skills I'd learn on the course would move everything up a gear. I was genuinely thrilled about the chance I'd been given.

I was dismissed by John just as the 'Supper's on the hatch!' call came from the kitchen. Despite pounding up the stairs even faster than normal I stood no chance of getting to the front of the scrum. The others would choose all the fullest of plates and I'd get what was left. 'Someone else has had their thumb in this,' I complained to Martin as I eyed up the final plate.

'Probably left a thumbnail in there for you, son. Best take it before we charge you extra for it.'

'What did the boss want?' Nicholas asked, goggle-eyed when I took my place at our table. I looked across the room. John, Joe and the other leading firemen were sitting at the far end of the room.

'I'm going on a course. To do cave and cliff rescues.'

'I can do those already,' declared Arfer, true to form.

'What, you're properly trained?' I asked dubiously.

'Self-taught. But I've got a good number of rescues under my belt. When I was in the merchant navy,' he began. A groan went up from what felt like everyone in earshot. 'When I was in the merchant navy I took over lookout duties almost every day. I could climb the masts higher and faster than anyone else on board.'

'Masts? What kind of ship was that? When were you in the merchant navy? Under Christopher Columbus?' asked Des.

'Backin' cheek. I climbed the Post Office Tower in London as well. Did it before you were born.'

'Did you help build the Pyramids, Arfer?'

'I could climb them. And let me tell you what happened when I was a long-distance coach driver . . .'

I tuned out as he began yet another endless story about jobs he reckoned he had done years ago. How much of what Arfer said on nights like this was true? Very little, probably. But it was all fantastically entertaining. It drew the rest of us together in a bubble of storytelling and gentle mockery. And it allowed me to drift away and dream about the climbing course. Three weeks today and I'd be there. I couldn't wait. What could possibly go wrong?

The first hint of disaster struck exactly a week before the course was due to start. On my days off I'd started working on a house in the middle of town, near the Golden Cross, one of the oldest pubs in the county. I'd stripped out the ancient kitchen from the house and installed something shiny and new. Now I was doing the same for the bathroom. I'd swung the lump hammer, sent up a cloud of dust and had a good time getting all the old kit out. The staircase was narrow and turned a couple of corners so I had to break things up to get them down – or bung them out the window into the garden. It certainly wasn't as easy getting the new bath up there when the time came. But the shiny new toilet and sink got in easily enough and were simple to connect.

At the time I barely even noticed the splinter that stabbed me in the side as I stretched out on the wooden floor to finish off plumbing in the bath. A couple of days later I got a reminder. It hadn't healed. It looked as if it had got infected. I tried to clean it up and forgot about it again. But two days later

– shortly before I was due to head off to Wales – it got worse. I woke up with an abscess the size of a table tennis ball on my side. I had a horrible feeling it might grow to be the size of an actual tennis ball by the time I reached the training centre in Wales. On a normal day it wouldn't have bothered me that much, but I knew that on the course I'd be expected to put on a full body harness and climb up and down who knows what, so something had to be done.

I decided to take myself off to casualty. They weren't too busy for once, and sorted me out without any delay. They took me into the treatment room and laid me down on an operating table, then gave me a jab or two to numb the area. To be honest I don't like needles and suchlike and wasn't looking forward to the imminent lancing, but my mind was taken off all that by the arrival of the nurse who was assisting the doctor that day. She was gorgeous, and after getting me ready, she sat herself on a stool to my right.

I'm almost certain she was unaware, but from where I lay I could see the top of her stockings, the place that Dave always called the giggle point, because once you'd got past that you were laughing! She easily kept my mind off what was going on in my side, and I used every bit of charm I might have had to make a good enough impression to perhaps ask her out on a date.

I was doing well, I reckoned. I was charming her; she was distracting me and then ... She dropped the bombshell. 'You're a fireman aren't you?' 'That's right' I said, my voice a little lower than usual. 'Perhaps you'll know my dad then – Bill Measures?' I was struck dumb. Bill Measures! Not Bill Measures, the hardest and most aggressive fireman in the whole of Shropshire who no one dared mess with? And this was his daughter?

I suddenly started taking uncharacteristic interest in what the doctor was doing and did my best to make light of my full-on chat-up attack on the lovely Kate Measures, who now had, in my imagination, a big 'Do Not Touch' sign hanging round her neck.

Finally the doctor packed the void he'd created with antiseptic tape and applied a dressing. I was done. I reckoned I'd eliminated the risk of getting into trouble with Bill after doing a lot of back pedalling, and I could get on with the job of hiding my dressing from the instructors on the forthcoming course so they wouldn't take me off it and send me home.

But at least the blinkin' thing didn't stick out so much it would stop me getting a harness on and doing the training. At least I got to go on the course.

It was wet, windy and far colder than it should have been when I parked my car at the outdoor pursuits centre in Plas y Brenin in North Wales. It was quite a basic place back then. I looked out over the collection of old slate buildings that spanned the Capel Curig to Snowden road and headed towards the one that looked as if it might have a reception.

It did. And it was filling up. There were twelve of us in total on the course. Each of the three fire stations in Shropshire had sent someone from each of its four watches. I knew a lot of the faces and quite a few of the names. I could sense that almost everyone there was as excited as me. This wasn't some course that we were being forced to do, it was something different, really physical and really challenging. It was every fireman's dream.

After a short wait we were sent to dump our bags in the dorm room and then to meet our two instructors. It was clear from the start that Mac and Ced were going to be good value.

Mac was a mountain goat of a man. He was tall, lean, strong – and impossible to age. He was described as one of the country's most experienced mountain guides. He had heavily lined, weather-beaten skin and wild grey hair. He never talked when he could shout. Ced was equally tall, lean and strong. He was a lot younger, probably about thirty. He was quieter. But he looked as if he might be a joker. And that suited us just fine.

The work – and the laughs – began straight away. The centre had an indoor climbing wall. It wasn't that high, but it went round all four walls of the room so you could tackle it from all sorts of angles. 'Right, let's see what you can do . . . round all four walls, fast as you can. Go!' Ced yelled out after we'd had our first few climbs. 'Bottom to top of each wall in turn. Go! Round the room, only using your arms. Go!'

I loved it. The whole thing was a brilliant blast of fresh air. It was like I'd gone back nearly five fantastic years. It was like I was eighteen again, brand-new and green as grass and happy as Larry to be in the Shropshire Fire Brigade at last.

Best of all was the camaraderie. Yes, it was serious business and we were there to learn. But you can't do that if you don't have a bit of mickey-taking and some fun as well, right? So it was no surprise that we had a few hairy moments winding each other up in all the worst places – like at the top of cliffs.

Back then the cliffs were real. We didn't do all the training inside. In fact, after that first morning, we did very little of it inside. We went up real cliffs. And we did it in all weathers.

'OK, I need a volunteer. You'll do,' said Ced at the top of our first cliff face.

He'd pulled forward a Shropshire lad called Vincent. About my age, Vincent had done far too much showing off on the course. So what happened next should have come as no surprise to him.

'You're going to be the first to abseil down,' Ced told him, passing him the harness and getting the rest of us in position to hold the ropes.

'I'm not going to slip, am I, pal?' Vincent asked nervously, as the rain continued to come down.

'Of course not. Whoops!' said the lad next to me, a guy called Sam, making a big deal of accidentally slipping on the rock – and dropping the rope in the process.

'Oh God, why me?' Vincent said. I'm not sure he'd have liked our answer, so we didn't give it.

Instead we got busy sorting out our anchor points. He tried to hide the fact that he was shuffling from foot to foot, nervously. 'I'm not going to look down,' Vincent said as Ced got ready to start the drill.

'Vincent, mate, it's your girlfriend!' Sam said, pointing over the edge of the cliff. Vincent automatically looked down.

'Bugger,' he concluded, looking pale. 'That's a hell of a long way down. And I'm serious. Don't slip. Don't let go,' he pleaded as we got ready for the off.

'We'll look after you, pal,' everyone lied.

And then the mischief making really began.

'Vincent, you want to make sure your gloves are on properly so you get a proper grip,' said Sam. He distracted him while Gareth, one of the men from White Watch, did a trick. He pulled the rope up a bit and created a loop in the line that was going to support Vincent. It's surprisingly easy to hold that loop, called a bight, even as the climber leans back and commits their full weight to it. A few moments later, when Vincent was doing just that and had passed the point of no return, Gareth released the loop. Vincent might only have fallen a foot and a half, but it obviously felt like a mile. He was right there, his head level with our feet when it happened. So we saw every

drop of blood drain out of his face. We saw every bead of sweat
– and heard every swear word too. Eventually, once everyone
had stopped laughing and he'd calmed down, he lowered himself out of sight and all the rest of the way down the cliff.

'I'll kill you all before this course is out,' he said when we
regrouped for the journey back to base. But in truth, he'd
redeemed himself and turned into a bit of a hero for having
handled the prank so well.

Jokes on the mountains aside, we worked on a lot of serious tasks too. A big part of what we learned was about anchor
points. Ultimately the whole set-up of a rescue is only as good
as the objects you anchored yourself to. So we explored all the
different ways you could use trees, rocks, posts or even cracks
in the rocks to create an anchor point.

When we climbed up the cliffs, doing real mountaineering
stuff, we learned how to put in protection using 'rocks and
chocks' as we edged up. 'These are pieces of metal shaped like
nuts – and I mean nuts and bolts, not hazel nuts,' we were told,
to general groans in the classroom. Out in the field these got
wedged into cracks before the line which was attached to us
from below was threaded through an attached karabiner, so if
we fell we'd not fall all the way to the bottom.

Last but not least came the next set of rescue exercises. We
piled back into the minibuses and Mac and Ced took us up to
another death-defying cliff edge.

'OK, team, you three will lower yourselves over the edge
of the cliff here with one of you bearing the stretcher,' Mac
began, while Ced took Gareth and positioned him halfway
down the cliff – or halfway up, depending on your point of
view and your head for heights. 'It's up to you how you secure
him and how you manoeuvre him to safety. But Cedric and I
will be watching carefully. And for the purposes of this drill

our casualty has broken several bones and is barely conscious. So best not to drop him, eh?'

We nodded and set to it. We dipped over onto the sheer, slippery rock face. We monkeyed our way down to Gareth, who was trying to win an Oscar shouting and screaming and pretending he was dipping in and out of a coma. We secured him to the cliff with slings, got the stretcher to him and then manoeuvred him onto it – all too aware that both trainers were now watching us through binoculars from below.

'OK, Gareth, do you feel lucky?' one of the lads asked as we released him from the first securing sling and the three of us continued to lower ourselves down, controlling the stretcher and casualty as we went.

'Blimey, pal, you want to eat a few less pies,' Vincent said when we finally got our surprisingly heavy casualty to the ground.

'Sorry, lads. I was told to carry this,' he said, dropping a hefty weight from the backpack on his shoulders. 'Mac didn't want it to be too easy for you.'

'Mac didn't want us to survive, more like,' said Vincent. 'I might write to my MP about this.'

'Well, you won't be writing any time soon, because the drill is not yet over,' said Mac, looming over us with his grey hair billowing in the wind.

'What now?' asked Sam.

'We go for a stiff drink at the Churchill Inn?' asked Vincent hopefully.

'Not quite. We don't do anything. But you carry your casualty, his stretcher and his backpack to the imaginary ambulance where first aid can more easily be given. And bearing in mind what I just heard, I think I may move the imaginary ambulance,' said Mac. He gazed out across the fields and pointed at a spot a horrifically long way in the distance. 'Off you go. Chop, chop!'

To be fair to Ced and Mac, they did give us down time as well. When we'd made it to the imaginary ambulance, gone back to the cliff to clear and pack up all our kit, we did get to go to the Churchill Inn. We even got to buy them both drinks.

The following day the first classroom topic of the morning was not the top of a cliff but the bottom of a cave. We crowded round a telly to watch a ridiculous video re-enactment about a rescue underneath some mountain in America. 'They gave it a Hollywood ending, by the way,' Mac declared as the screen went black at the end. 'In real life two of those men died. Only one of their bodies was ever found. You've got half an hour for lunch. We're going to the caves at two p.m. on the dot.'

Part of the plan on those early cave exercises was to see how claustrophobic we were. Which was quite a lot, in many cases. In the process we also discovered how vain some of us were. Miles, one of the old-timers from Wellington station, was bound to a stretcher like a missile on one of the first simulated rescues we did at the caves over towards Llanberis. He lay there, trussed up like a turkey, as we prepared to lift him.

'It's going to be tight,' Gareth had shouted out, not particularly reassuringly. And so it was. The stretcher had to be carried through a very long, very narrow and very low passageway to freedom.

'Watch my nose! Don't bash my nose! I don't want a broken nose!' Miles shouted every time the stretcher came close to the rocky roof of the tunnel.

We were equally naughty on the stream course – a long tunnel that has about six to eight inches of water running through it when the water table was at normal levels. The day we were there the water was flowing fast and furious. It swirled around in the blackness. The bubbles and the turbulence meant you couldn't see what lay beneath. Which gave us an idea.

'Every here and there a particularly hard volcanic rock will have wedged in a dip in the floor,' our trainer barked at us in the classroom. 'It will tumble over and over in that dip. And as the centuries pass it will wear a very large hole in the stream floor.'

'How large?' someone asked.

'The worst of them can be five feet across and ten or more feet deep.'

Interesting.

'Mac will lead you and let you know where the worst of those hazards are,' we were told. Mac had turned up for the morning's session in a particularly bad mood that day. He'd growled his way through the first safety presentation and dealt with all the other classroom learning at a rate of knots. Then he'd got us all kitted up in the proper outfits for pot-holing, which was really nothing more than tough plastic overalls, wellingtons and a waterproof torch on our caving helmets.

We made our way to the cave entrance and headed into the darkness. The sound of rushing water got louder with every step. It echoed off the stone walls. You could smell and taste the dampness – and probably the excitement and fear as well.

'Right, follow me,' Mac yelled, before yomping through the water at a rate of knots. 'Hole ahead! Feel for it with your feet!' he yelled a few minutes later. We all tried to see what he meant amidst the gloom. 'It's here,' he said, pointing at an area that looked no different to any other. Then he wedged one foot on each side of the cave. He lifted his arms to gain some traction and support from above. Then he walked, legs apart, over the hazard.

'Windsor, you're next,' he shouted and watched me follow his lead to the other side of the hole. 'Tell the next man in line about the technique then follow me,' he said.

I did so. I powered further into the cave. 'Hole ahead!' he yelled at another point. We all repeated the trick and continued into the wet, echoing darkness. Or at least most of us did. At the back of the group was poor old Barry. He was a good lad, but a bit of a whiner. He'd been whining for Britain all morning. He'd been moaning about feeling tired, being hungry, missing his bed at home. So he needed a wake-up call.

'This one here is the biggest hole in the system,' Mac was saying. 'You need to get both feet on one side of the tunnel and put both hands on the other. Then sidestep your way across,' Mac yelled. I watched him do it and followed suit. The three guys behind me did the same. But where was Barry?

'I want my blinkin' lunch! Can't we just leave him here?' Vincent asked, glad that the joke wasn't on him this time.

'Of course you can't leave him. But you could forget to tell him about the hole,' said Mac.

'Hurry up, mate, it's time to get out of here and have some grub,' Vincent called into the cave behind, where we could finally see Barry's head-light approaching.

'On my way. Sorry about the wait,' he said as he got round the final corner and strode towards us all.

Then . . . Suddenly he disappeared entirely from view. All we could see, refracted wildly in the swirling water, was the light on his helmet. We fell about laughing and this continued every time we remembered his dunking.

'Bastards, total bastards,' was all he could say when he surfaced. It was all he did say for the rest of the day, I seem to remember. Fair enough. But at least he knew what the rest of us knew. The Fire Brigade was an equal opportunities employer long before that phrase got invented. We'd take the mickey out of anyone. And the next day it was Sam.

His bad time began when we were taken down to something called the Worm Hole – a particularly narrow twenty-foot tunnel deep in the Welsh hills. 'It's tight and it's cosy down there,' Mac told us ominously.

It certainly was. Most of us were big guys, so it was quite a squeeze in places. Sam, who was particularly barrel-chested, had the toughest time of all. 'Come on, pal, just a bit more,' we shouted to try to egg him on.

'Push a bit more and it does get a bit wider towards the end. You'll make it,' we said.

He did. 'I don't fancy trying that again,' he told Mac when we all regrouped and debriefed at the end of the day.

'Well, you don't have to. We'll not be going down the Worm Hole again. Tomorrow it's the Anorexic Worm Hole. Sam, you'll be first. See you then.'

That night we wound Sam up as tight as a tick.

We ate and drank pretty well on the course. Big hearty dinners were served in one of the slate buildings – which were functional rather than comfortable in those days. Then we would walk down to a local pub with a bunch of other people who were in the centre doing a variety of different courses. So there were always tall tales to tell and to hear.

Sam survived the Anorexic Worm Hole, though it was a close thing. And we all survived the week. The course had a final exam, but we were pretty much talked through it in the classroom. All the real assessment had been done out in the field, the way things always used to be in the Fire Service. Mac and Ced clearly felt that all twelve of us could lead a team and help save a life or two. If we'd not been up to scratch, I don't think they'd have hesitated for one second in telling us so.

And how fast did the week go by? Well, very fast! It shot by. I loved every minute and I'd have happily done it all again. But I was equally keen to head on back to base. We'd been given lots of brand-new cliff-rescue kit to take with us. Our new helmets and gear were stashed in kit bags so we could lob everything onto the station Land Rover and head out to wherever we might be needed. Call me a big kid starting a new chapter in his personal boy's own adventure, but it was fantastic. Just fantastic.

# 14

# Catching Up

'Come on then. What have I missed?' I shouted out the question. It was the start of a raucous fireman's supper on my first shift after the course. We were on nights. And everyone was more than happy to fill me in.

'What have you missed? What have you missed? You missed the fact that Simon nearly lost us the fire engine!' crowed Charlie with an even louder giggle than usual.

'It was not my fault,' Simon shouted back from the next table. We still sat four to a table in a long line across the messroom floor. I got the impression that Simon had been offering up that same defence for some time. As if it was going to make any difference.

'What's not your fault?' I asked him.

'What happened outside.'

'So what did happen outside?'

'He crashed the water tender ladder!' Charlie said with another gleeful giggle, cutting through what was in danger of becoming a decidedly circular conversation. 'No more than four hundred yards away. He took out a Rover 2 Series.'

Simon took up the tale. Everyone was listening now. I was agog to hear it for the first time, but I'm sure the rest of them wanted to know whether he was going to change his story. This is going to be good, I thought happily.

'I was heading south and a car was in front of me,' he said. 'There was plenty of room for everyone. As long as everyone acted sensibly.'

'Like you've ever acted sensibly in your life!' said Des.

Simon got the back of his hand to the back of Des's head – and not quite as good-naturedly as normal. 'The car had indicated right, but it pulled in to the left. It slowed down and all but stopped. He was doing the sensible thing. He was letting me past.'

'And . . .?' I asked.

'And he must have decided at the very last minute that there was time to get across. It was rank madness. But he might have made it. If he'd cut the corner, he'd have turned into the road and out of my way in time. But another car was coming up the road from the roundabout. The idiot in the Rover had nowhere to go. He couldn't cut the corner and he froze. He slammed on the brakes and we slammed right into him.'

'You slammed right into him,' Des corrected, still rubbing his head.

'It was pretty bad,' continued Simon, suddenly rueful. 'We're a nine-tonne weapon in the ET. He was in a Rover. The whole back of it was shunted up about four feet. The back bumper was on the back seat. Thank God there was no passenger there. That wouldn't have been a joke.'

'Where were you heading?'

'To an RTA on a lane down south over by Hope Bowdler. We had to get the next nearest ET to take over.'

'So Simon's on probation.'

'I am not and it wasn't my fault. Anyway, I did less damage than you did in September.'

Des winced. We all did, to be honest. We'd been sent to some distant field out in Dorrington. We were there to tackle a crop fire – or a standing corn fire as we were unaccountably being told to refer to these sorts of incidents in the future. They can be brutal events. You don't want a fire when the corn has stopped growing and started drying. You don't want it when the sap has gone and there's plenty of room for air to collect between the stalks. But that's when these fires happen. Careless walkers or horse-riders, people smoking at a picnic, farmers' machinery setting off sparks . . . Plenty of things can trigger fires at harvest time – and a host of other factors can make bad jobs much worse.

That September day over on the A49, most of the usual factors had come into play. It had been a still, hot and heavy day. The air was as dry as the corn. The unusually large field in question was wide open to the elements on one side and had a row of thick trees on the other. It was the perfect layout to pull the air in from the easy side, feed the fire in the middle and push the air up and away by the trees. In a nutshell, I suppose the conditions created the ultimate crop-destroying machine.

Heat rises, of course. As it does so it draws in air from around it. On some occasions it can suck in air with so much force that it whips up the fire and creates a self-perpetuating firestorm. Throw in some thermal activity, that bubble of warm air created by the fire, and whole invisible clouds of air will be on the move upwards. I knew about this from my times in a hang-glider. I knew how columns of warm air can force you up and down with incredible, unavoidable strength. I knew that once all this funnelling of air began it wouldn't stop.

We were already sweating cobs up on the WRT as we got ready to fight what felt like a living and breathing fire. Des was driving that day, and after getting us on site fast his next responsibility was to park in the safest, most effective place. That's vital in a wide-ranging, self-perpetuating crop fire. They can move faster than any of us can run. If the driver is not at the wheel and in gear, they can also move faster than a fire engine with all its hoses out.

'This is a big one!'

'You tackle it from the edges over there. We'll start from the other side,' Joe had yelled. He was busy marshalling the rest of our manpower as Des opened the levers controlling his hose-reels and engaged the pump so the water began to flow. We'd barely made a dent when the next wave of hot winds gave the fire a hell of a lot more life. It roared up. It crackled and cackled and exploded all around. You could sense the change in the whole dynamic. The fire had taken on a life of its own. It seemed like it wanted to show us who was boss. Like it wanted to beat us. So it pulsed and pulled in more air and doubled up on itself. It also started to move. Fast. In next to no time it was racing towards us. And it began to roar towards our fire engine.

'Des! Get it out of there!' Nicholas yelled. He'd been brand new on the watch back then, but he'd been closest and he'd spotted the danger first. He'd won a lot of much-needed Brownie points that day.

Funny, but as the fire sped up, everything else seemed to slow down. From the far side of the field I remember watching Des fly into the cab, fling it into gear and jerk fourteen tonnes of appliance and kit towards safety. The hoses yanked out of our hands as it went. Nowadays, safety mechanisms mean you have to disengage the pump before a truck can move. Thankfully not that summer, though. The hoses bounced along the ground, spurting water all over us, our heads and in our faces.

'I did it, though, didn't I? I got the engine out of harm's way. It didn't get as much as a scratch. I knew what I was doing. I don't know what you were all so bleedin' worried about,' Des said.

'We were worried about the long walk home if the truck had gone up in smoke.'

'We were worried about all the report writing we'd all have to do.'

'And we were worried about deciding what to do with your body after the Chief Fire Officer got his hands on you, most likely,' said Pete.

Des was on the point of saying something – or at least he looked as if he was – when he got saved by the bell.

Charlie's anguished sigh was ringing in my ears as we abandoned our dinners, flew out of our chairs and headed for the pole or the stairs. A fire had been reported in a flat on the outskirts of town. Our job, of course, was to put it out. Though we were about to find out that the flat's very angry owner had other ideas.

The property address was in a modern block in the centre of Shrewsbury. On our way we passed St Chad's Church, where the town had recently had its Hollywood moment. Three years ago they'd been filming *A Christmas Carol* in the town. The graveyard was the site of a fake gravestone for Ebenezer Scrooge.

'That'll be a tourist attraction for years,' Charlie had declared at the time.

'It'll be gone in a week,' Woody had said.

So far it had lasted three years and counting. St Chad's Church itself, of course, is worthy of visitors in its own right. Shrewsbury is a town of spires. It hosts a clutch of beautiful church buildings including St Mary's. The medieval buildings in the heart of the town rightly get plenty of recognition too. But they're not our only jewels. We've got Lord Hill's column, supposedly the highest Doric column in the world and a fair bit taller and fatter than Nelson's version in London. And if you want to see where skyscrapers were born then come to Shrewsbury. We might not have the ancient towers of San Gimignano in Italy. We certainly don't have anything like the ones in London or New York today. But if you want to see where the experts say it all began then come look at our now-derelict Ditherington Flax Mill, the world's first iron-framed building. It might be only five storeys tall, but by all accounts it showed builders what could be done. Eat your heart out Empire State Building, we've got your grand-daddy right here in glorious Shrewsbury.

Of course for all the beauty and the history we also have our share of modern eyesores. We've got concrete too. There's Lloyds Bank in the High Street and the New Market Hall, which plenty of locals detest. Then there was the modern residential block we were heading to that night.

The fire was up in a top-floor flat, we'd been told. When we pulled up, the usual goggle-eyed neighbours and local shopkeepers were in the street, gazing up at the smoke pouring out of a couple of windows. The police were there, keeping order, and an ambulance was right alongside us, just in case.

As the danger was obvious from the off, we all got set to tackle it fast. We hit the ground, ready to play our separate parts. I was working alongside Martin and we were fully kitted up in our BA sets to get inside the property and do whatever had to be done. Though first we had to get up the outside staircase and in through the front door.

'I'll lead you up. And you could have a problem,' shouted the police officer, a po-faced man in his mid-forties by the name of Norman. John, as the officer in charge, came along to find out what he meant.

'It's one more floor. And get ready,' said Jocelyn, the other police officer on duty, as we met her at the top of the second stairwell.

We passed her in a blur. The hose-reel was heavy and the fire kit is hot. But even in the rush I wondered what she meant. 'Get ready!' It was a strange thing to say. If it was a warning then it was an odd one. As a fireman, you're always alert to danger. You always expect the unexpected. Of course we were ready. What was going on here?

We made it up the final twist of the staircase. It was obvious which flat was in trouble. A cluster of people were standing at the far end of the corridor looking towards it. And smoke was seeping out from under a small frosted bathroom window.

Norman thundered past us to disperse the crowd. 'How many times have I said it? How many times? Get away from here,' he was yelling.

Meanwhile Martin and I hammered on the front door. That was us being courteous, I suppose. We always hammer on doors for a moment or two. Then we break them down.

'Fire Brigade! Open the door!' Martin hollered.

With no response he gave me the nod. We were getting ready to force it when events took us by surprise. The door swung open. A huge cloud of smoke mushroomed out towards us. And a big, angry-looking man in jeans and what had once been a blindingly white polo shirt took up a ridiculously firm, square-footed stance in front of us.

'Fire Brigade!' Martin said again, as if it was necessary.

'Piss off,' said the man whose house was on fire.

'Get out of the way. We need to get in,' Martin declared.

'Are you deaf? I told you to piss off.'

'Your house is on fire. Get out of the way or we'll move you out of the way.' This was getting interesting. The smoke was thickening now. This place was in trouble. I edged forward in the narrow stairwell. I wanted to be right up there if things kicked off.

'Move me? Move me? You want to try it, pal. This is my house and you are not coming in.' The man swung out a thick arm to slam the front door shut, but Martin swung out a foot to keep it open.

'Is there anyone else in the house?' This was the serious part.

John was up at Martin's side by this point. And we were all facing a dilemma. Technically, we're not allowed to man-handle members of the public. That's the job of the boys in blue, who have that thing called powers of arrest. But they can't go into a burning building because they don't have that thing called breathing apparatus, which we do.

We hurried back to the outside steps to decide on our options. While we had been inside the building, two more police cars had arrived containing some beefy-looking policemen. When we told them of our encounter, one of them said simply, 'You wait here, we won't be long.' Four of them ran up the stairs, along the corridor and banged on the door. The man inside opened the door, ready for another rant, but before he could utter a word he was grabbed, and dragged shouting and struggling into fresh air and down the outside stairs before being literally sat on by two officers while a third put on the handcuffs.

If they hadn't done what they did, he could have died. The smoke had gone well past the danger point. He'd not be standing up for long. Everyone's bravado disappears when they can no longer breathe.

Now Martin and I could do what we're paid for and check that the flat was empty and put out the fire.

By the end of it a good time had been had by all. The fire had started in the living room, probably by a pile of laundry, though that was for others to work out. It had eaten up the curtains, along with a load of other kit, and taken a big chunk out of a toxic-smelling sofa.

'An old friend of yours, was he?' Martin asked Jocelyn once we'd finally got the job done and were back in the street.

'We know him pretty well,' she said with a rueful smile.

And a few weeks later we found out more about what had gone on that evening. The man's girlfriend had been one of the crowd in the street when we'd first arrived. She'd come over and identified herself to some of the watch while we were upstairs tackling the fire.

'He lit it. He set it off. He does this sort of thing all the time. He wants attention,' she'd said to Dodger.

'He wants locking up,' Dodger had replied, not unreasonably.

At the time she'd agreed. 'I'm going to leave him. I can't live like this. He's a danger. And I've got a kid.'

But a couple of weeks later we learned something else. Nicholas had met one of the local coppers in town and got the inside gen. The guy had finally admitted to lighting the fire himself, saying he'd done it to show his girlfriend who was boss. He'd wanted it to burn as long as possible to teach her some sort of lesson or punish her for something or other. Then, maybe, he'd planned to put it out himself so he could play the hero and win her undying affection.

'What a tosser! There's kids living in that building. She had a kid herself, didn't she? People could have died if the fire had taken hold. What a total idiot,' Dodger said.

'That's not the best bit,' Nicholas said. 'You know how she told us that he was a danger and a liability and that she was leaving him? You know she said he was always doing stunts like that and it was the final straw? Well, she's only gone and forgiven him! She's sticking by him and she's taken him back. She won't give evidence against him. She's swearing blind that she caused the fire herself by leaving an electric fire drying towels when she popped out to the shops or something. She's happy to take the rap herself, if needs be. We put that fire out for nothing.'

'We should have evacuated the building then left the dipstick in his flat to burn,' said Dodger.

The rest of that morning passed in a mix of drills and, for me at least, a bit of daydreaming. I had a lot on, away from the station. Like most of the men I had a second job during my time off. I did all manner of building and DIY work. I was almost totally self-taught, picking things up as I went along, or reading up on them in my *Concise Repair Manual* before doing a job for the first time. I never felt ashamed of asking others for advice. And in the Fire Service you've got a whole host of practical men to turn to. Most are only too willing to sound off and let you know how good they are at things. Charlie and Woody did painting and decorating and we worked alongside each other on the occasional job. John had his own, much bigger building concern. Martin did a spot of plumbing, Gareth and a couple of other guys on Green Watch did electrical work, and almost everyone could turn their hand to carpentry. The floats we all made for the Shrewsbury Raft Race could put Notting Hill or Rio to shame.

I'd recently taken on my biggest job to date, a huge kitchen and bathroom refit and general maintenance job at a house near my old school in Harlescott. The man who owned it said he could swing a lot more work my way if I wanted it. But did I want it?

I enjoyed the challenge. I liked the extra cash. But I had other things on my plate as well. I'd joined a drama group when I was fifteen. I'd always loved being on stage and I'd thrown myself into the hobby, the way I threw myself into most things. It had been brilliant fun from the start – even though I did get into a lot of trouble with the first play I directed.

It was called *Housekeeper Wanted*, and I'd taken the lead as I was the only drama group member of the right age. I'd managed to juggle the rehearsals and the performances round my shifts. We entered it into a competition in Telford. The audiences and judges liked it. And we got nominated for an award! The presentation was going to take place in Telford on a Saturday night – a Saturday night when I was supposed to be working. I took a sickie. I'd never done it before, and I've hardly done it since. But at nineteen that award and the rest of the drama group really mattered to me – and I couldn't think of any other way to get to the ceremony.

'This had better be worth it,' I thought as they announced the winner. It was. We won. And in that moment my cover was blown. A photographer from the local paper was there to record this local lad done good. The picture went in the next issue. The caption said what I'd won – and more importantly when I'd won it.

'Malc, Joe has read the paper. He's gunning for you,' Woody tipped me off when I ran into him in town ahead of our next shift. So I grabbed a medical dictionary off the bookshelf at my mum and dad's house. I read and memorised the symptoms of gastroenteritis. I parroted them to my GP, with a suitably grim expression on my face – and I was a prize-winning actor, after all. He wrote me a back-dated sick note.

'You were off sick and yet this newspaper proves you were at a fancy event in town,' Joe began.

'But I was ill.'

'You weren't too ill to dress up and collect some fancy prize?'

'No, but I sat right near the toilet the whole evening. I only left that chair to get the prize and have my picture taken, then I was back outside the toilets. I was too ill to come in and risk going out on a shout,' I said. I paused before playing my final card: 'Here's the sick note from my doctor.' All the wind suddenly went out of Joe's sails. He hadn't a leg to stand on, so he gave me a mute stare and stormed off.

I'd got away with it. Though I'd done nothing like it since and had only gone for small parts in our subsequent productions. Two years on, should I throw caution to the wind and try to play another lead? We were auditioning for Prince Charming in a big pantomime production. I sat in the station that afternoon and imagined what it would be like to play that part.

Then I moved on to another daydream. An even nicer one. I'd met a girl called Karen, who was the sister of one of the girls in a group I led at church – something else that took up a lot of my time. She was away at university and had only been back for a quick visit, but I'd taken a fancy to her. I wondered when, or if, I might see her again. I hoped I would. As it turned out, we did see each other again. In her long summer holidays she taught the piano. So I asked her if she'd teach me. We talked as we played. We became friends – and we took things slowly. It was some time before I went so far as to ask her out, but once I did it was only two years before I married her and we started our lives together. But even back then, having only seen her across a crowded room, I had a feeling she was going to be special. So I daydreamed about her at the station and smiled as I worked.

# 15

# Anyone for Turnips?

The call came through at the end of the afternoon. And it was a tad confusing.

'Why do they need us to move thirty-five turnips?' Nicholas asked, quite reasonably, as we got ready for the off.

It turned out that most of us had misheard the brief. 'It's not thirty-five turnips. It's thirty-five tonnes of turnips,' John said irritably.

We nodded as that sank in. 'That's a lot, right?' Woody mused. 'A hell of a lot.'

And so it was. We headed roughly north towards Market Drayton, another jewel box of a local town with more than its fair share of half-timbered old buildings and ancient red-brick houses. If we'd got as far as its main street we would have passed its fourteenth-century sandstone church – and given a nod to the old fire bell in the Buttercross, a stone structure in the heart of town. The bell was there to commemorate our equivalent of the Great Fire of London. The Great Fire of Market Drayton had come about fifteen years before London's version in the seventeenth century.

'The fire began in a cake shop,' Charlie, of course, was wont to say if ever the town was mentioned. 'And when everything was rebuilt properly, do you know what they invented here?' he would ask.

'Gingerbread,' we'd say, like a chorus of bored schoolboys.

'Gingerbread dipped in port. Or was it rum? Either way, I say it put any of Charles Darwin's discoveries in the shade. He might be everyone else's local hero, but he's not mine. Evolution is all very well, but gingerbread and booze? That's true genius.'

Standard conversations over, we continued heading north on the Market Drayton road, crossing a honeycomb of small fields and passing through the copses, dips and dales that litter the county. A few moments later we found out we were close to our destination.

'Are you lot heading to the overturned trailer? You'll laugh your heads off when you see it,' a motorist shouted up at us after flagging us down. 'The driver says he misjudged the corner. There's a heck of a camber down there, right enough. He did everything wrong and ended up tipping the trailer onto its side. I've just turned around and I'm going to find another way through. I can't see you clearing it any time soon. Best of British to you all. You're going to need it!' And with a cheery toot of his horn he was gone.

We carried on for a few more minutes. A couple of other drivers waved at us as they too headed the other way. Then someone in a jet-black XJS Jaguar flashed his lights and got us to stop a second time.

'It's a disgrace what's happened down there. I'm late getting to a very important meeting and now I'm going to have go miles out of my way. You should have been here a long time ago to clear this up. Why exactly have you taken this long? What do I pay my taxes for?'

'We're answering the call right now, sir. We were informed about this incident less than fifteen minutes ago.'

'That's fifteen minutes too long. It's a disgrace. This country is going to the dogs. It's going to hell in a handcart,' he said. Then he too drove off. No cheery toot of the horn from him.

A couple of minutes later and we'd made it. And there they were. Turnips. Thousands and thousands of the things. They seemed to cover every inch of the road. It was the strangest roadblock I'd ever seen. And one of the funniest.

'When all else fails, call the Fire Brigade,' John muttered under his breath as we climbed off the engine and surveyed the scene.

'You'll break your backs doing this, gentlemen,' a nearby motorist shouted out. 'I've thrown about twenty of the buggers into the ditch and it's nearly broken mine. They're heavier than they look. And they're four feet deep in places.'

John let out a low laugh as he continued to survey the scene. 'I don't think this could possibly have happened in a worse place. It's like it's been done deliberately. Deliberately to make us work ten times harder than we need.'

It was easy to see what he meant about the location. On any ordinary, wide, flat road most of the truck's payload would have rolled into the verge of its own accord. On a narrow lane raised up a little or on a slope, many of the beets might have rolled out of the way quite naturally. But this jack-knife had taken place in one of Shropshire's hidden hollows. The narrow road turned at the very base of the dip. Steep grassy banks rose up on either side of the road. There was nowhere for the turnips to go. Six deep? I'd have said at least twice as much. It was as if a giant vegetable avalanche had swept down the valley and cut off the village.

At that point we saw one of our local police officers, whose car was parked on the other side of the blockage, making his way towards us. He was walking, very, very unsteadily, on top of the shifting sands of turnips. The sheepish-looking lorry driver who had caused all the mayhem was staggering equally uneasily in his wake.

'Bit of an unusual one for you gentlemen,' the policeman said with a rare smile. He was an older officer called Patrick. We knew him well from various shouts around town. To be honest, he wasn't that easy to get along with. He had a serious manner and insisted on things being done right. It was obvious he didn't approve of the way we took the mickey out of each other on occasion. But even he couldn't see this as anything but bizarre.

'I dunno what happened. I just dunno. I was telling the inspector here, it happened so fast,' the driver said in a rush.

We were all smiling at that comment. And Woody decided to twist the knife.

'What inspector?' he asked.

'This one. This inspector right here,' said the farmer.

'Oh, you mean the constable, here,' said Woody, trying not to smile.

Seeing that Patrick was looking even more humourless than usual, John defused things by moving the conversation on. 'You're not injured?' he asked the driver.

'Not a scratch, sir. But I injured my pride, right enough. I've cost myself a fair bit of money on the trailer and everything that was on it. But nothing more than a scratch on me.'

John sighed, shrugged and then turned to face us. 'Well, it's not rocket science. Let's get to work.'

And so we did. It was hilarious, really. There we were, a team of fully kitted out firemen, all trained to the hilt, forming a human chain and chucking vegetables up a hill and out into a field at the top.

'Here's your starter for ten, Windsor. Catch!'

'Over to you, Woody. Catch!'

'And to you, Charlie.'

'You're last in line. Don't let us down and drop it, Beardsmore. Catch!'

Most of the time, fortunately, we did catch what was thrown at us. Though we did throw in a fair few googlies and low bowls when we got bored and felt like a bit of variety.

'Who eats turnips nowadays anyway?' asked Nicholas at one point. 'Where are they being sent to? Russia?'

'It's only animals who eats them. We're doing all this for a bunch of cows,' hazarded Woody.

'No we are not. You can make some darn fine food with turnips,' said Charlie, defensively. 'Neeps and tatties – who doesn't like those? Or add them to some creamy mash or cook them with butter, brown sugar and a little syrup. You can eat them raw. They're very refreshing grated up on a salad, so I've read. Or cook them with apples. Or with carrots. Top them with a nice thick cheese sauce and you're laughing. Animals indeed! There are dozens of uses for these little beauties.'

Hunger pangs aside, it turned out to be a fantastic shout. It was physical stuff. You couldn't kick or roll the things up the hill and out of the hollow – not without breaking your foot at least. They had to be thrown man to man, one at a time. If we'd thought hard, I'm sure one of us could have come up with a builder or farmer pal who had access to a fork-lift truck or something. But that would have spoiled it.

I for one was enjoying myself. The late afternoon sun held low and steady in the sky over to the west. It had been a clear, fresh autumn day. There was moisture in the air. It tasted alive, somehow. It reminded me of long walks in the woods as a kid. It was bonfire time, one of my favourite times of the year.

As we all stood up straight and took one of our periodic breaks from being a conveyor belt for vegetables I looked along the line and realised I wasn't the only one having fun. Robin and Woody were in their element too. This was like an extra workout for them. A fresh-air gym – on work time.

The only people who weren't happy were the occasional motorists who came down the lane and saw the blockage. 'How long have you been at it, then?' we were asked by one of them.

John looked at his watch. 'A good hour,' he admitted.

'Not got far, have you.'

The man had a point. 'Are these things actually self-perpetuating or self-replicating or something?' Des asked. 'Are they reproducing, or is some turnip gremlin creeping in and putting a new one on the pile for every one we shift?'

'Well, they certainly won't be gone by knocking-off time. Best get on the radio,' said John.

And a little under an hour later we were relieved of our duty. So this agricultural emergency hadn't seen just one set of kitted-out, fully trained firemen picking up turnips. It saw two of them. Green Watch clocked on back at base and then headed out in the station minivan to relieve us. Funny how all the different watches seem to lead parallel lives. We all do the same things and we all know huge amounts about each other, but we rarely spend any time together. We rush past one another when we start and end shifts. When we get together for occasional parties or events we tend to stick to our own teams. But if I'd worked anywhere else, I reckon Green Watch would have been a decent team to be on. They were a mixed bunch – we all were, I suppose – but they seemed to find life as funny as we did. They took the good and the bad of the job in their stride. They balanced out the highs and the lows, the pleasures and the tragedies. They kept their sense of perspective and humour. They needed it that autumn evening.

'We thought it was a wind-up,' one of them admitted when they arrived.

'Windsor and I are fully trained mountain rescuers now. We shouldn't be wasting our time on jobs like this,' said Gareth, who I knew well from Wales.

'Well, you're all going to be wasting your time till about midnight, I'd say,' said John.

We wished them luck, did the official handover of duties and kit and headed back to base fast. They kept the fire engine – so they would be ready to get to a real emergency if one came in – while we squeezed into the minivan they'd arrived in. It was crowded, sweaty and more than a tad whiffy.

'What's that smell?' Robin asked at one point.

As if we didn't know.

'Turnips,' said Charlie, with one of his biggest giggles. He had somehow stashed half a dozen into the van while no one was watching. 'I'm in the kitchen when we go onto nights next week,' he said proudly. 'This is going to be a big part of your dinner.'

# 16

# Lucky Drivers

∞

Charlie was first to hear about it. 'It was up north. In Exeter,' he began, after Maggie had served up another vast fireman's lunch and we'd got our heavily laden plates back to our tables.

'Exeter's not up north. Not unless you're French,' Woody pointed out.

'Might have been Exmouth,' Charlie admitted.

'Are you French?' Woody persisted. 'I bet you'd eat frogs' legs if you had a chance. And dogs. Don't they eat dogs in France?'

'I think that's Thailand. Or China. Or is that cats?' mused Simon from the leading fireman's table at the end.

'Look, forget about China and frogs' legs for half a minute. A lorry crushed a car in Exmoor,' Charlie shouted, an unusual amount of frustration in his voice.

'Lorries crush cars all the backin' time,' said a bored-sounding Arfer. 'You'll have to come up with something better than that if you want anyone to keep listening.'

'It is better than that. Just blinkin' listen!' said Charlie. So we did. 'It was in the early hours and it was pitch-black. The lorry came up to a traffic island somewhere.'

'Ex-Ditton?' interrupted Woody, before admitting he'd made that one up.

172

'It hit the camber on the island and it toppled right over. It hit the ground with a heck of a thump, by all accounts. The driver got out without much more than a scratch. He said later he'd been tired, a bit sleepy and he'd maybe been driving too fast. Anyway, he was wide awake then. So he stood about for a while, hoping to flag some car down to get help, but there was no one around. So he legged it to the nearest town to find a phone box. He called it in and the police said they'd pick him up on their way to the scene. When they got there everything was exactly the way he'd left it. They got the Fire Brigade out and everyone tried to work out how they were going to right the thing.'

'I'd have done it by calling out the heavy recovery lads and sitting back and watching someone else sort it out. It would have been job done in half an hour, leaving plenty of time for a nice full English by the end of the shift,' said Simon.

'Well, it didn't go as smoothly as that. Because someone heard something.'

'What?'

'It sounded like a voice. From a long way away. But the police thought it was probably a fox or an owl or something.'

'So what did they do?'

'They got ready to right the truck when they heard it again. And that time they recognised it. It was a voice. Voices. Two of them. Coming from inside the truck.'

'People-smuggling? The slave trade? Cattle-rustling?' ventured Woody.

'Was it the backin' Child Catcher?' asked Arfer, who I suddenly realised was starting to look increasingly like the Child Catcher himself.

'Well, the police had a bit of a go at the lorry driver. They accused him of all sorts. They said he had to have something or someone in the back of the artic. He swore he didn't. So they opened it up to take a look. It was packed with boxes.'

'Boxes of what?'

'Packing materials, or so he said. He was on a regular delivery. It was what he did every week. Nothing ever changed. He got the artic loaded up with box after box of packing materials at the depot and then he headed off. No people, no animals, nothing but rolls of wrapping paper, cardboard, insulating foam and the like.'

'So the boxes were haunted, right?' said Simon, trying to sound bored and sarcastic. He was probably jealous that Charlie of all people had held the floor for so long. We'd all ploughed through our inch-thick lamb chops and boiled potatoes by then and we'd not even got up for seconds. Even Maggie was leaning in, over the serving hatch, to listen to the story.

'Well, the police pulled the first few boxes out to see if anyone or anything was inside them. It was still dark so they got the squad-car lights lined up to see inside.'

'And in the distance a lone owl hooted and a cloud covered the moon,' said Simon sarcastically. Everyone, including Maggie, told him to shut up.

'Half a dozen boxes later and they'd not found anything unusual. But they could hear the voices even louder. They were definitely voices. A man and a boy. The police got it straight away. They said there had to be a car under there. But the lorry driver swore blind that there wasn't. The road had been empty when he'd toppled over. There'd not been a car in sight. The road was always empty at that time. He'd not seen a single car pass all the time he'd waited and walked back to find his phone box. There was definitely no car underneath his lorry. Except that there was.

'They got a load more of the boxes out. And by then they

couldn't miss the voices. The boxes and all their contents had muffled them. The cardboard and the foam had been perfect sound insulation. And when enough of them had been moved and the boys in blue got their car lights shining in the right direction they could see it. Inside the overturned lorry, sticking through the curtained side of the trailer was a perfect car-sized, car-shaped bulge. My pal said the outline was totally intact. It was like a *Tom and Jerry* cartoon.'

'So there had been a car trapped there all along? Those poor people! It doesn't bear thinking about,' said Maggie.

'It was a man and his son,' Charlie continued. 'They started shouting for help like nobody's business once they realised that someone was there. The cops radioed for an ambulance.'

'And what were our boys doing all this time? Why weren't they in there straight away to sort it out? What were they doing, waiting for the cops and the medics? Lazy bleedin' buggers,' said Joe from the far corner of the room.

'They did get stuck in, in the end. It's my mate in Coventry who knows someone who works there who told me all this. They're not bad lads, up there in Exeter.' We let that geographical detail go, this time. 'They cut through the tarpaulins and there it was, hey presto, barely damaged and with hardly a dent. A sky-blue Ford Fiesta.'

'That's a dreadful car,' interrupted Martin. 'Handles terribly. Rusts like a bucket, I reckon.'

'And what about the poor people inside it?' Maggie persisted.

'Our lads cut right down the side of the car. The doors opened easily enough, by all accounts. Just needed an extra pull and twist. They both got out. Barely a scratch on either of them.'

'So what did the lorry driver say?' I asked.

'He said nothing at first. He was dumbfounded, my mate

told me. He kept saying there'd been no car there, nothing on the road. He couldn't believe it.'

'And what did the car driver say?'

'He said it had been like a bolt from the blue. One moment they were driving along, minding their own business. He'd been going to Portsmouth or somewhere and his lad had come along for the ride. The kid had been half asleep.'

'How old was the poor lamb?' asked Maggie.

'A teenager, I think. Maybe fifteen.'

'Bless his heart.'

'So, like I say, one moment they're driving along, the next moment a bloomin' lorry lands on them. He said it happened faster than he could blink. They were stopped dead. And everything went black. They were covered, enveloped – they were totally hidden. It was like they were in a tomb. He said he thought at first he'd gone blind. And they had no idea how it had happened or what was going on.'

'They didn't shout for help?'

'They say they did. But no one heard them. And after a while the lorry driver had buggered off to find a phone, of course. He was gone for a good twenty minutes. The man thought it was the end of the world. He thought they'd been abandoned, somehow. He said he didn't know what to think.'

'And they couldn't hear out, the way no one outside could hear them,' I said, piecing it together.

'They couldn't hear a thing. They had no idea whether there were ten people come to help them or none. It was only when the boxes started to move that they felt the vibrations and started to shout again.'

'What a story. That poor young lad,' said Maggie.

'And this is true? It's not one of your tall tales?' asked the more suspicious John.

'Every word,' declared Charlie. And he got rewarded for his trouble. Maggie made us all wait while he got the pick of seconds.

We were still picking over the bones of the story that afternoon when our next call came in. It seemed we had an equally lucky driver on the country roads of Shropshire. These things really do come in twos. An extraordinary battle-axe of a lady called Fenella was about to share the father and son's good fortune.

The call said her car had gone off the road in one of the worst possible places in the county – on The Burway, the narrow track that hugs the edge of Carding Mill Valley. The area is known as Shropshire's Little Switzerland. It is a truly beautiful part of the world – so beautiful, in fact, that I swear Switzerland should face facts and accept the description of Bigger Shropshire.

We were on the A49 sixteen or so miles south of Shrewsbury – the stretch that runs through Church Stretton, the historic spa town that boomed in Victorian and Edwardian times. We passed the old train station on the main street that used to greet rich visitors in the steam age. Up ahead of us houses hugged the hillsides and scrawny sheep mooched around on the muddy fields.

Driving up The Burway was like doing a high-wire act, with the Long Mynd hill above you on one side and a slope that resembles a cliff falling away on the other.

Dear old Fenella had been heading up that road late in the morning when something had gone wrong and she'd veered off. But not into the soft earth of the hillside to her left. No, she'd gone to her right, heading off and over the edge of the cliff. Cars do that, every now and then. Their stories rarely end well.

We were expecting the worst as we parked the engines where the churned-up gravel showed she had begun her unexpected journey.

'Bloody hell, that must have hurt,' Pete muttered as we looked a long way down.

'If this were a Hollywood film, there'd be a fireball down there,' said Des.

Funny that. In all my years I've never seen a car explode the way they do in the movies. But while Fenella had got lucky on that score it didn't seem possible that she'd survived the descent.

We were about to start the climb down the muddy, stony slope when the ambulance crew arrived. They normally beat us to scenes like this and it's always good to have them around.

'Bloody hell, that must have hurt,' the main medic said, holding out a hand and introducing himself as Dominic as he joined us looking down at the half-crushed car.

'Those were my words exactly. Absolutely exactly,' said Pete.

'Who called us all in?' Dominic asked.

'Another driver who saw it from behind. He hot-footed it into Church Stretton to find a phone.'

'Do we know who's in the car? Or how many of them there are?'

'Not yet. We've been shouting, but no reply.'

'That's not good,' Dominic said, adding a surprisingly loud holler of his own.

And that was when we heard Fenella for the first time.

'There is absolutely no need for anyone to shout at me,' came a stern, female voice from the body of the stricken car far below us.

'Can you hear me?'

'Of course I can hear you. Do you think I'm entirely deaf?'

178

'Are you hurt?'

There was a pause. The voice, when it came, seemed angrier in reply. 'Why would I be hurt? What a fool you must be. I simply need a little help with my car.'

We looked at one another. We had sped up our descent five-fold after hearing her voice, clambering over rocks and bushes and scree until we were almost there. The car, a Renault Clio had clearly taken some hefty knocks on the way down. It had then jammed itself into a mound of earth and a pile of rocks ahead of us. The bonnet looked to have been prised up in the impact like an old sardine-tin lid. The amount of glass and other debris that had scattered – and the distance over which it now lay – suggested that the descent had been very bumpy indeed. And the woman inside thought she needed a little help with her car! That had to be the understatement of the year. Her only option once we got her out would be to sell it for scrap.

'Can you give us your name?' Dominic yelled as we made our final approach.

'Of course I can.'

Silence ensued. For some reason I understood where this lady was coming from faster than any of the others.

'*Will* you give us your name?' I called.

'It's Mrs Fenella Street.'

I allowed myself a smile. She reminded me of one of my teachers, also a stickler for good grammar and good manners. 'My name's Malcolm. Malcolm Castle from Shrewsbury fire station,' I said as we finally got abreast of the car.

Mrs Fenella Street was sitting bolt upright in the driving seat. Both hands were firmly on the steering wheel. Most of her well-coiffured hair was still in place, though one thick strand had flopped down over her left eye, which I could tell was annoying her hugely. The lady was wearing a seat belt. Not everyone did, back then. Older drivers were particularly bad at using them. But the seat belt had surely saved this lady's life.

'Somebody called the Fire Brigade?' she said in response to my greeting. 'What on earth for?'

'I'm from the Royal Shrewsbury. We're here to check you out and get you looked over,' interrupted Dominic.

'The Royal Shrewsbury what?'

'The Royal Shrewsbury Hospital,' he said, flashing me a look of confusion.

'And you are . . .?'

'From the hospital,' he repeated. He was about forty and he was looking a little nervous all of a sudden.

Seeing a disapproving look flash across Mrs Street's face, I prompted in a classic stage whisper: 'She wants your name.'

'I'm Dominic Hobson.'

'Well, Malcolm Castle and Dominic Hobson I'm aghast at how much money this must be wasting. I shall raise the matter with someone at my earliest possible opportunity because it seems entirely excessive. I am perfectly well. But I do, as I say, need a little help with my car door.'

# 17

# The Flying Boot

∞

Six days later, Martin and Simon made Charlie a very happy man by cooking up a real fireman's dinner – brick-sized portions of steaming lasagne with veg and garlic bread followed by sweet rhubarb crumble with our obligatory thick custard.

'Custard's out of a tin, but you can't have everything,' Charlie whispered as he dug deep with his spoon.

'What's that, old man?' an angry-sounding Martin yelled from the kitchen. He clearly had excellent hearing.

'Nothing at all. I'm tucking in,' replied Charlie.

When all the bowls were scraped and licked clean we had one of our usual water fights washing up and then hunkered down for the evening. Nicholas had been sent down to the ice-cold study room on the middle floor to do revision like I'd done six years earlier. John was down in his office and Woody had his feet up on the desk in the watch room. Martin had moved on to a second set of wrought-iron gates and was sending sparks flying in the workshop. A couple of the guys had braved the cold night and were tinkering with their cars outside. It was calm, companionable and perfectly normal. Everyone always seemed to have some project or other to be getting on with.

I'd bagged one of the comfiest armchairs in front of the

telly, though I was supposed to be learning my lines for my drama group's panto.

All around me the mess room was filling up. The bar was open and had been busy since the shutter went up. Joe was drinking his bitter and smoking a pipe while I had a lager. Most of the other lads had pints and everyone was happy. By the time it got to eleven, John had made it upstairs, the car cleaners had come in from the cold and the workshop was silent. Only Nicholas was still downstairs.

The canaster school got going. There was no money involved but a whole lot of pride was always at stake. A little later four of the usual suspects started playing poker for pennies in the corner, the way they always did. Those games could get intense at times, but overall the night was a typical mix of light-hearted joshing and calm, companionable drinking. Or at least it started out that way.

Who knows why these things kick off? But put a dozen or so big, highly charged, competitive blokes in one small place and kick off they will. Especially when there's this much cheap drink involved. Funny the way your sense of how much you can safely drink always goes in reverse proportion to how much you actually drink.

We took turns working behind the bar. We'd look after it, taking the money, cleaning the pipes and stocking the shelves. But mostly it was Pete's manor. He was a born publican, a born barkeep. He loved being behind the bar. It was his favourite job. And he was always jumpy when someone else was in his spot. And that night Gerry was pulling the pints and taking the cash.

Their argument must have begun earlier on. I'd not had sight nor sound of it, but I soon got wise.

'Idiot, effing idiot,' Pete was saying under his breath. He had a tough, sharp face, our Pete. His eyes were dark and never still. He was always itching for a fight.

'What did you say?'

'Effing idiot,' Pete muttered again, in a low, angry voice that Gerry would have struggled to hear.

'What did you call me?'

'The way you lord it about back there. Throwing your effing weight around. And you don't know the first thing about a bar. You couldn't run one if your life depended on it.'

It wasn't clear who, exactly, Pete was talking to. No one was really listening. But we could all hear. I could certainly sense the tension rippling through the room. A storm was about to break.

'You want to get over here,' Gerry growled from the bar.

'Not worth the effort,' spat Pete, louder this time.

'Let's take it outside then.'

'You're not even worth it.'

'Well, shut the eff up.'

'Make me. I'd like to see you try!'

So Pete did try. For some bizarre reason he decided to throw the first thing he could lay his meaty hands on. Which turned out to be one of his shoes. He picked it up, swung back his arm and aimed right at Gerry's head. But that wasn't what bothered me – or any of the others who'd looked up fast. Gerry could look after himself. What bothered us was what stood behind him at the bar. The line of optics that were paid for by our booze money and subs. Every type of drink was lined up. There had to almost a month's worth of booze there. Smash that and the start of World War Three was all but assured.

Gerry's eyes were ablaze as he got ready to face the airborne assault. He wasn't normally a swearing man but he let out a stream of expletives that night. Over to his right, in a chair by the window – and in what felt like slow motion – John stood up. The blood seemed to be visibly draining from his face as he tried to assert his usual control. But there was no time. Pete let rip with the shoe. It shot across the room like an Exocet missile. Gerry just about had the time and the gumption to duck. The blood had drained from all our faces by then. Because with Gerry out of the way, our booze was looking very vulnerable indeed.

'That, my friend, was close,' Martin whistled by my side. I shook my head in agreement. By some stroke of incredible luck the shoe had slammed into the square of hessian and mirror right in the centre of the line of optics. It knocked off the photo of the big-breasted lovely on the cardboard that held all the packets of peanuts. But it didn't smash a single bottle of booze.

Not that this would stop World War Three.

Gerry threw himself over the bar – not a bad manoeuvre for a man his age and size – and powered across the room towards Pete. Another crisis seemed to be on the cards. Pete was standing bang in front of our brand-new rented TV. If he got pushed backwards and smashed into the screen, all bets would be off. We'd be fighting so much the whole station could catch light and we'd still not pull a punch.

'Leave it, Pete,' Woody yelled, lunging towards him and trying to set up a personal demilitarised zone.

'Leave it, Gerry,' John shouted, lunging at the man closest to us.

Nevertheless, fight it was. Despite all our best efforts, Gerry and Pete had managed to meet in the middle of the room. The first punches were thrown as John, Woody and I piled on top of them and tried to grab their arms. A mass of other bodies rolled in from all sides. And there we were. At least half a dozen of Shropshire's finest, mildly pissed and scrapping like schoolboys.

Gerry and Pete – who, incidentally, had not long started working alongside each other in a brand-new plumbing business they'd set up for their time off – were trying to get in as many punches as they could while the going was good. They didn't have long. The rest of us prised them apart and dragged them to opposite corners of the room.

'Unbelievable! In the mess room. Unbelievable!' John bellowed as he began the mother of all dressings down. He got them on their feet and out into the corridor. He read the riot act to them for starting a mini-riot of their own. Then, after a long, loud tirade, he led them back into the room.

'Drink to it?' he asked, now that calm had been restored. Gerry and Pete did. We all did, as it happened. Because there's nothing like alcohol to calm down arguments in the workplace, right?

Half an hour or so later the poker game was back on in one corner and the canaster players were getting intense in the other. Gerry was buried behind a classic car magazine while Pete had resumed control of the bar and was mopping away at the surfaces like a man possessed. Woody was marking out likely cars in *Exchange & Mart*, Nicholas – who had poked his head round the door to see what all the fuss was about and been told to forget his books for the night and have a pint – was now sitting alongside Ben and Joe watching *Match of the Day* on the telly we'd saved from destruction.

It was then that it hit me: this madness might not last. The fire station bar was the heart of our on-duty world. It was where we spent so many of our working hours. We took turns running it and we talked endlessly about extending it. There had never seemed to be any rules over who drank what – or how much. Bearing in mind that we went off to drink-drive incidents on a regular basis, it was ironic that our allocated drivers, though they might drink a little less than the others, still drank.

We sobered up fast if we had to. It was amazing how completely we changed when the alert call came over the tannoy system.

'I'll have a word in the morning,' John would state, portentously, when anyone crossed the line and got so pissed that they had to be sent to bed to sleep it off.

But still we did it. We were big guys, so we could probably hold more booze than most. But six or eight pints a night was the norm. Then there was the other stuff. George and Howard, two of the old-timers who'd recently retired and who had been in the Fire Brigade for longer than I'd been alive, had been big whisky drinkers. Brian, a brick wall of a man, seemed to almost single-handedly keep the makers of gold label barley wine in business. He could knock back two or three in the first hour and a half after dinner. But surprisingly he never seemed to get drunk.

Could all this carry on? My mates outside the Brigade said it couldn't. They could never believe the stories I told about life up in the mess room.

One of them, who worked for a bank over in Telford, probably put it best: 'We've got a sports club right out on the edge of town,' he'd say. 'We get special membership rates and we can go there for a game of squash or something after work. After the game there's a bar where you pay normal prices and have a few drinks before going home.'

'Sounds all right,' I'd say.

'But you've got an actual bar, right there in your station.'

'Yes, in the mess room.'

'And it's subsidised.'

'We run it ourselves, so it's cheap. We cover costs rather than make a profit. It's sort of wholesale prices or mates' rates.'

'And you can drink whenever you want.'

'Well, it's only open in the evenings.'

'But it's open when you're on shift, when you're working?'

'Yes, we're the only people there in the evenings.'

'Incredible. You've got the best job in the world!'

I wasn't ever going to argue with that. But I knew it couldn't last. We'd long since heard the stories about a watch in London, or maybe it had been the southwest of England, where the guy driving the fire engine had been forced to take a breath test after an accident. He'd failed, and failed badly. Newspapers had been full of stories about drunken firemen. Readers weren't impressed. Our unions were strong and fought change like rats in a trap. But this had to be battle we'd lose in the end. So much of the madness, and the fun of the work was fading. The anarchy of fire station life was being organised out of existence. John and Joe were always moaning about the latest forms to be filled in, the latest paperwork to complete. Were our new recruits subtly changing things as well?

I looked across to where Robin was ignoring the car and bike magazines and reading some health and fitness title. He wasn't drinking. Robin had been with us for about six months now and he was casting an interesting shadow – and not merely because of all the weight-lifting he did. Yes, he'd laughed along with the rest of us over Charlie's ever increasing obsession with food. But he'd not shared it. He'd actually taken to suggesting ways to make our grub healthier and leaner. All this had horrified Charlie, of course. But Robin had got Nicholas and even Woody interested. Some days he'd bring in his own muscle-building supplements and sit with

Tupperware containers full of pasta at dinner time. A couple of the guys were starting to follow suit. The old cry of 'Dinner on the hatch!' wouldn't be the same if half of us were obsessing over protein and calories.

'What's up with you, Windsor?' Pete asked, breaking into my musing. 'You look like a man who needs another drink.' I smiled and took one from him. I had a couple of packets of salt-and-vinegar crisps put on my slate as well. If the world was changing, I might as well enjoy it all while it lasted.

# 18

# The Haunted House

Our team had a crunch volleyball match the following evening at the start of our night shift. We were in a league at our local sports centre over in Sundorne. We made royal progress over there in a procession of fire engines. We parked them in the car park and left our full kit on the seats so it would be ready if we needed it. One man was left in one cab to listen to the radio for any messages from Control. Then the rest of us ran inside to try to beat the heck out of Blue Watch.

Lately our league games had got pretty good. All the happy brawls we had back at the station had hardened us up. With a bit of focus and tactics, mostly brought in by newcomer Robin, we had shaped up into a point-scoring machine. We were almost manically competitive. But then so were the guys on all the other watches.

A decent crowd turned out to watch our games. Most of the spectators were friends and family. Others were passers-by and centre-users attracted by the noise and the sheer ferocity of our games. And we were worth watching, though I say so myself. We made it personal and we really went for it. I wasn't alone in thinking I'd rather break my leg than let the idiots of, say, Blue Watch win a match against us.

The other reason we were worth watching was because we could sometimes spring a surprise on the spectators. If we got a call in the middle of a game we were out of there within seconds. That's when we snapped back into duty mode. No matter what had been happening, no matter what the score was or who had the ball, half the people on the pitch would simply leg it out of the building and run towards the fire engines in the car park. The ball would bounce away, forgotten, into a corner of the court. Our opponents would stand there, never quite sure if this counted as a win, a loss or a draw.

We got away with this provided we did indeed get out of the building, onto the engines and out on the shout as fast as we could have done from the station. That was a maximum of thirty-three seconds for a day shift and no more than fifty-three seconds when we were in bed at night. We reckoned we could meet the thirty-three-second target from the sports centre. We'd probably smell a bit, but we could be kitted up and ready for action on time. We'd be on the road just as fast.

That night we didn't have to test the theory. No calls came in. The guy in the fire engine cab sat there, smoking, reading the paper and listening to what was going on in the rest of Shropshire on the Fire Service radio. Those of us inside on the court lost the game, sad to say. But we'd had a blast. So we were all fired up for the evening – and all ready for the potential madness of a country night shift.

We had our huge meal. We got up to the usual juvenile antics while we were washing up. We had the banter over what we would watch on the telly. We badgered each other for cigarettes, saw some curious darts games begin and felt the mounting tension over poker games played for pennies.

'You know what, lads? You're the worst company in Shropshire. I'm off to my bed,' said Dodger shortly after midnight.

I tried not to let my smile show. We really were like schoolboys sometimes. We always made fun of the first person to go to bed each night. There was some macho rite of passage about staying up late. So if you wanted to get a decent night's kip you had to wrap it up in big fat slice of sarcasm.

'The party always begins when you leave the room, Dodger. Good backin' riddance,' said Arfer.

'There's a nasty surprise tucked away at the bottom of your bed. Sweet dreams,' threatened Gerry.

Offering two fingers up to the room, Dodger disappeared through the door.

On night shifts John got a prison-like cell of a room to himself. The Sub-O and the other leading firemen shared a room. The officer on watch got to lie on a roll-down bed in the watch room downstairs – though he was supposed to stay awake. The rest of us piled into the dormitory on the first floor right below the mess room and the bar. It was closed off by a set of thin plywood folding doors – and the newer you were to the watch, the closer you had to sleep to the doors.

'Dodger's right. You're a bunch of losers. See you in the morning,' I said half an hour or so later. No one so much as looked up. It was only the first to bed that got noticed.

My bed was over by the far window and the radiator. I placed my clothes and boots were exactly where I expected and needed them to be at my side. You don't want to waste a second if a call comes in. Then I put my head down. It's useless trying to predict whether you're going to get a call or not on any given night. But sometimes you want a quiet night more than others. As a keen-as-mustard jockey on the watch I'd wanted a call every night, just so I could test myself again and again in as many new situations as possible.

Nowadays, with so much going on in my life, I could use the sleep. Sod's law dictated I wouldn't get it. And I didn't.

The call came in a little after 3 a.m. 'Attention!' boomed the voice over the tannoy. Then the tones played. Everything's automatic when you're woken on shift. As I say, you know exactly where your clothes and boots are. No one touches anyone else's stuff – unless some joke's going on. We weren't joking then, in the thick, cold darkness of a November night. You pull on your trousers and shirt. You slip on your shoes. Then you race across the dormitory floor and out to the pole, sprint through the muster bay and into the appliance room, on to the vehicles and out within those vital fifty-three seconds.

As I did it that night I was reminded of one of my first-ever night calls. It had been in the summer. I'd been so keen, so worried and in such a hurry I'd not had time to do up my shirt buttons before I hit the three-and-a-half-inch-diameter steel pole. Let me tell you, few things hurt as much as slamming down a stainless-steel pole with your bare skin against the metal. I might not remember much from my school physics. I might not understand how a bar of metal can get so hot, so fast. But I knew friction when I felt it and I felt it then. The wheals took nearly a month to heal. The others had taken the mickey out of me mercilessly for ages afterwards.

That night, some seven years later with enough buttons firmly done up, we'd all got down the pole unharmed. We piled onto the appliances within the required number of seconds. Then we hit the road. The streets in the heart of Shrewsbury were all but empty. There were no people walking around and few cars on the road.

I looked out of the window from my seat in the back of the cab. Shrewsbury was always like a ghost town in the wee small hours – not least because it was so old and it looked as if spirits really could rise from those medieval buildings. In the half-light, spirits could surely reclaim the very streets they had built.

And ghosts returned to my thoughts when we got to our destination. The old hall we'd been called to could figure in any Hollywood ghost story. It was a vast Victorian or maybe Edwardian pile. Or maybe it was Tudor. We're lucky to have a lot of places just like it amidst the villages of Shropshire. Whatever it was, we swept up between overgrown hedges on a long, wide drive. We shuddered to a halt in the gravel outside a vast front door. From outside it was your classic country house, one that had survived centuries of history and had now suffered several decades of decay.

The night was clear and the moon was near to full as we jumped out of the appliances. There were no street lights this far from town and no lights in the Munster Mansion ahead of us. With no roads around there were no car lights either. But the moon and the stars were bright. They cast some surprising shadows, for the angles of the building were augmented by a set of new, incongruous shapes. The builders were in. Having been derelict for some time, the hall was currently being converted into flats. Towers of scaffolding loomed large over sections of the building.

'I'd like to be doing this job myself,' I muttered, taking in the scale of the building work. 'It'd pay me enough to retire.'

'If you were doing this job yourself, Windsor, it would have fallen apart long before now,' John declared.

I was trying to come up with a witty reply when some sort of caretaker or security guard approached us from the end of the drive.

'It's damn kids,' he said, spitting a glob of phlegm at the rough, weed-infested gravel driveway. 'They come in here every blasted evening, messing around, taking stuff, setting everyone back. They use the place as some kind of playground. As soon as we boot them out, they come back in. The police don't want to know. Lowlifes, most of these kids are. And to-night they beat everything. They thought it would be funny to set fire to the blasted place. They started it right there in the main hall, by the look of it.'

He was pointing towards the centre of the building. With so much metal, wooden and plastic sheeting on the doors and windows it was hard to see inside. It would have been easy to drive past this place and not realise that there was a fire there at all.

'If I see the kids again, I'll kill them,' the man declared.

'I'll help,' said the child-hating Arfer.

'I don't think so,' said John, our voice of reason. 'Now, let's take a look and see how bad it's got. What's the best way in?'

The caretaker gestured towards the chained-up corrugated-iron door that stood where once something far grander had been. 'Key's right here,' he said, handing it over.

We got the door open and looked inside. It was pretty bad. The kids had found plenty to burn. The vast open hallway was stuffed with builders' kit and rubbish. There were tall piles of new and rotting wood, stacks of cardboard, paper, plastic – you name it. The fire had been set at the far end of the hall near the foot of the staircase. Some of the stuff had burned fast. The fire must have given off a lot of heat and travelled to the rest of the stuff, the piles of damp, rotten materials. These presented us with a different problem. Here was the ultimate slow-burn scenario. And it was pumping out clouds of dense, acrid smoke.

This old building is more watertight than it looks, I thought as we finished off our initial examination. There didn't seem to be many openings for the smoke to seep through. So until we tackled the fire, and created some ventilation, it was going to be particularly hard to see and to breathe inside.

I was on the rider board to have my breathing apparatus on alongside Gerry, one of the old-timers. We got ready, got the hose reels out and pushed our way through the ground floor of the building looking for the source of the fire and the main areas to which it had spread. It was incredibly hard to see. And what the fire lacked in hot flames it certainly made up for in thick, billowing smoke.

We aimed the water at all the key points. We can alter the shape of the jet of water coming out of the hose-reel branch to send out more or less of it. That night we went for a fine jet to give the place a short, sharp initial assault. At that setting we could hit the centres of all the seats of fires we came across. Unless there are other, otherwise unknown factors at play, it does the business fairly quickly. It got the job done that moonlit night. We found and hit all the visible flames. Then we moved around the entire hall, checking. Although visibility was still lousy, the fabric of the building didn't appear to be under threat. The only things burning had been the building materials and decades' worth of junk. A lot of the wood in old buildings like these tends to be of the hard, dense variety, like mahogany. It took a lot for this to catch light, and thankfully it hadn't happened here.

Gerry and I gave the hallway a final dousing then headed back outside to give John an update.

'Visibility is practically zero but we're pretty sure we've got the worst of the fire taken out. We got here in time. It's not spread,' Gerry said as we laid down the hose-reel.

'Well, if you see any of those kids, aim that water right square at their faces,' the caretaker shouted from where he was loitering near the cab.

'I think that would get us arrested,' Gerry said with a laugh.

'I'd swear in court it was self-defence. Or an accident. Those blighters deserve all they get.'

Fortunately for them, the blighters were nowhere to be seen.

A couple of minutes later, Gerry and I were dispatched back into the building to try to do something about the smoke. Inside the main hall, right by where the worst of the fire had been, there was one of those vast, grand staircases. It curved and was wide, high and, fortunately, made of huge amounts of fire-proof stone and marble. We had a long way to go.

As we yomped up the first few steps, a shape caught my eye. Was it a carved, stone pineapple on the balustrade? What was that all about? I made a mental note to take a closer look on the way down. We carried on stomping up the stairs. Our kit was heavy and hot, but at least there was nothing particularly challenging about our task.

Smoke rises, so we were in the situation that surprises lots of people – that the further up we got from the fire, the thicker the smoke became. After checking for any residual fires we pushed onward and upwards. We were planning to head on up to the top floor, where we'd open as many windows or sky-lights as we could find, to let the accumulated smoke escape.

The fifth floor looked to be the top, which was good news as we didn't fancy climbing up any more stairs. This was a high-ceilinged building. It had at least a couple of dozen big stairs between each floor. Fortunately, right ahead of us was a single small skylight. It was exactly what we were looking for. Except it was too high to reach. We looked around for some-thing to climb on, but there was nothing around. No rocks to lob through the glass either, though we'd only have done that as a last resort. It brought back the memory of a shout during my first year on the brigade, when a pal chucked a fire-damaged electric heater out of the open second-floor window of a country mansion just like this. He'd not realised it was still plugged in. So it had immediately arced back towards the building and smashed through an ancient, no doubt priceless, stained-glass window on the floor below. Probably best not to make the same mistake here, I thought. But with visibility still terrible, we needed to find a way to ventilate this building fast.

The obvious thing to do was to go into one of the bedrooms to open a window there. Gerry and I stomped down a wide landing. After about fifty feet we came across a huge, probably stained-glass and probably ancient window looking out onto the grounds. Better not throw a stone through that, I thought. What I could see of it was beautiful. If it hadn't been for the smoke, I imagine the moonlight would have streamed through it, drawing faint, coloured pictures on the bare wooden floor.

All the doors off the landing were closed tight. Our training and our experience teaches us to treat things like this with a degree of caution. You never know if the fire has built up on the other side, for example. So you try to find out before opening a door and giving it the extra oxygen it might be craving.

'Checking the door,' I heard Gerry mutter as he felt for hot spots and did a quick handle check. Gerry can't have felt anything that night. He reached down again and turned the handle. He pushed the door open. Then he leaned forward and prepared to head inside in search of a window.

At that point I was right on Gerry's tail. You stick close to your buddy when you're in smoke as thick as this. His life is yours and yours is his. The whole point of pairing up is to be each other's eyes and ears. It's what we have drummed into us in all the drills we carry out on the drill ground. The purpose becomes clear when your visibility and your hearing falls to almost zero. Somehow, amidst the swirling black smoke of that huge, ancient landing, my eyes saw something that Gerry had missed. Or, more accurately, they didn't see something he'd missed. They didn't see a floor on the other side of the door Gerry had opened.

He was mid-stride when I moved. He was on his way into the room, pivoting on his back foot, going forward. I don't think he could understand my words of warning. It was muffled by the BA mask and all our kit. But he felt my arm. I grabbed and gripped him so hard he flinched. I pulled him back so strongly he fell. And he weighed fourteen stone if he weighed a single ounce.

'What the hell are you doing?' he shouted out as we hit the ground on the landing.

We could communicate a lot better than we'd done in the past because we were equipped with the new 'Interspiro BA sets' that had a refined speech diaphragm in front of our mouths. In truth it was nothing more than a vibrating metal disc in a sealed unit, but it worked it well enough when it came to sharpening up the muffled sounds that made it through the BA set. So that day I could hear Gerry's words loud and clear as he swore at me in confusion.

'I saw something,' I said. I got to my knees and inched past him to check I'd not made a stupid mistake. Was I right? Had I imagined the danger? I was right and I'd not imagined a thing. Gerry pulled himself up and stood next to me at the door. He swore and he whistled. Both sounds echoed through the Interspiro set into my ears. We weren't standing on the threshold of a room at all. We were standing on a ledge. There was no floor to the bedroom on the other side of the open door. Nor were there floors to any of the bedrooms on the five floors below us. This was one hell of a building project! They had gutted every inch of the body of this place. They'd left nothing but the spine of stairs and the landings.

'That's got to be fifty feet down,' said Gerry, awestruck.

'You wouldn't get up again if you fell down there,' I agreed.

'How did you know? Why didn't I see it?'

I shrugged. 'I don't know. There was something – a sliver of light. Something in the smoke that didn't look right.'

'How come we didn't see it from the ground floor?'

'We wouldn't have been able to see the ceiling, even if there had been one – the smoke was so thick.'

'If I'd done one more step I'd not have got back up,' Gerry said, echoing my words.

Standing in the doorway, on the edge of the ledge, we suddenly started to laugh. Up there in the thick smoke and the danger of the darkness we laughed like idiots. We laughed so much and so loud we fell over for the second time. We knelt on the landing, gasping for air as the relief hit us both.

Then, when we'd recovered, we stood back up.

'Un-chuffing-believable,' Gerry said. Then he punched me incredibly hard on my shoulder. So hard I had a bruise for days. That was how we said thanks, back in the day.

'There's no floors up there, not a single one. The building is like a skeleton,' Gerry yelled out to John when we got down to the main hall. Then he caught sight of our caretaker friend leaning on the side of one of the appliances, chatting to some of the other lads. 'You!' he bellowed. 'You didn't think to tell us that there were no floors in there? You let us go up and didn't tell us? We could both be dead, you understand? Dead!'

The caretaker, to be fair, didn't try to duck out of it. He started to swear like you've never heard. 'I never thought. I just never thought. I didn't know you were going up there. I thought you knew. I'd never – never. I'd not. I'd not,' he mumbled, running out of steam and words. Then he found the ones he needed. 'I really am so effing sorry,' he said.

It was enough. We got some kit from the lockers on the appliance and headed back into that vast, smoke-filled interior.

'You'd never know. You can't tell,' I shouted out when we crossed the hall and looked up. The smoke enveloped us. You couldn't see that there was no ceiling at the far end. You'd never think it or guess it. You'd just assume it was there.

We yomped back up the hundred or so steps to the top floor. We got the lone skylight open at the rear of the landing. Then we managed to get a pole through one of the bedroom doors to open up a window above a missing floor. Down below, the others were pulling planks and sheets of iron away from doors and windows on the ground floor. The worst of the smoke immediately began to mushroom its way to freedom, billowing out of the old hall and into the night.

For some reason I could picture the scene as if from above once we were outside. A vast old shell of a house, with its windows open and thick black smoke billowing out of them. It was weird. And yes, a little spooky.

It turned out I wasn't the only one to be thinking those thoughts. 'Remember that house over in Pitchford?' Woody asked when we'd re-stowed our kit and told the others, probably with suitable embellishments, how close we had come to dying.

'There's a lot of houses over in Pitchford, soft lad,' said John.

'The one the police wouldn't dare go in.'

John let out a laugh. 'Oh, that one! The police were the soft lads there, true enough. Girls' blouses, the lot of them. Always were. Always will be. Emergency service, my left foot!' he said with a wry twinkle in his eye.

'Steady on. They're not that bad.'

'They were that night.'

'So what the hell happened?' asked Robin.

Woody settled himself down in his seat and launched into the story. 'It was an ugly old house. An old farm cottage from years back. Deserted. Abandoned. Had been for some time. Wasn't bothering anyone. Not the best neighbourhood out there. No one cared if one more front garden was full of old junk and the lawn never got mowed.'

'But they cared when they started to hear the ghosts,' John interrupted with a laugh.

'Indeed they did. They heard ghostly rumblings. They talked about spectral moans. There were balls and chains being dragged around, by all accounts. It was the Princes in the Tower – right here in rural Shropshire. A posse of neighbours – not one under the age of seventy, to be fair – got themselves all worked up and made the call.

'Ghostbusters?'

'No, us. Well, the police, to start with, to be strictly accurate. The local lily-livered boys in blue blouses turned up. Got out of their Z-car and got as scared as all the old-lady neighbours. So they called us. They called the real men at last.'

'What did you find?'

Woody took control of the tale again. 'A world gone mad. Everyone hysterical. Neighbours all wobbling like custard – and that was just the men. All of them coming up with every type of ghost story you could imagine. Talking of calling the vicar, having an exorcism, saying it was the end of times, confessing their sins.

'And all in a tumble-down farmhouse on the outskirts of a town that time forgot. If I was a ghost I'd find a hundred places to haunt before I haunted there. Not that this cut much ice with the old ladies – or the police. They said the house had always been trouble. They said the last owners had disappeared in the night. There one day, gone the next. A family of crims, according to the coppers. But a clear case of ectoplasm or something, according to the old ladies. Anyway,' Woody said, leaning back in his seat and relishing the rapt audience, 'we decided to get on in there. We marched up the front path, looked in all the windows, listened at all the doors. And blow me if we didn't hear it ourselves. There were chains clanking away in there. Ghostly moans as well. It was the Hammer House of Horror, right enough.'

'It was badgers,' John interrupted, spoiling the whole story. 'A set of badgers. They'd taken up residence and were having a bit of a party. I got a sight of one from the kitchen window. You couldn't miss the smell when we finally got inside.'

'I thought badgers were supposed to be clean animals?' said Gerry.

'Not these ones,' said John.

'And the point of the story,' said Woody firmly, clearly furious at missing the chance to deliver the punchlines himself. 'The point of the story is that we're the best of the best. We get a result when everyone else fails. We go where others fear to tread.'

'Even to a nest of badgers. You heroes,' said Robin, brave enough to be sarcastic.

We settled back in the cab, satisfied with our prowess, as the shadowy Shropshire countryside flashed by the windows. We passed a village of what looked like flinty stone buildings. They glistened in the moonlight. High stone walls crowded in on us as we drove through. They had clearly been built in a bygone age. They'd stood there when highwaymen had ridden through the night. They'd soaked in the sound of horses' hooves and mail coaches. What did those walls think of us, this procession of massively heavy, gleaming, modern vehicles? They'll be here when we're long gone, I thought suddenly, not sure if that was good or bad.

'On the subject of ghosts – don't forget that our Woody here can raise the dead,' Gerry said, bringing me out of my own thoughts with a jolt.

'Oh God no, not that bloody story again,' Woody moaned.

'He raises the dead. But he screams like a girl in the process,' Gerry continued.

'I might have let out a short cry of surprise.'

'You screamed like a girl.'

'It was years ago in Longdon Coleham,' Woody began, clearly thinking it would help if he could get his side of the story told first.

'The neighbours said an old woman had died in her house,' said Gerry, determined not to let him. "They said she'd not been seen, not been picking up her local paper, not bringing in her milk. They'd banged on the doors and shouted through the windows. One of them got her phone number and they tried to ring her. Nothing doing. So they called the police and said she must be dead.'

'The police saw a half-open upstairs window so they called us to get a ladder up to it,' continued Gerry. 'It was a small window so we sent our smallest, weediest man.'

'We sent our leanest, wiriest man. Not the one with the beer belly that's as big as the butter mountain,' Woody corrected.

Gerry patted his beer belly with something akin to satisfaction. 'Anyway, up the ladder he goes and in through the window he gets.'

'It was dark as anything. No street lights, no moon, nothing. I turned on my torch and headed over towards the light switch.'

'What happened?'

'What happened is that I straight away saw the dead woman on her bed. I shone the torch in her face to see what was what. And she only went and woke up,' he said.

'She screamed her head off!' roared Gerry. 'And so did Woody!'

'Maybe, just maybe, I made some sort of noise,' said Woody. 'And I defy any one of you not to have done the same.'

# 19

# Where's Norris?

'Well, Windsor, it looks as if one of your mad mates has got himself into a bit of a pickle,' John said as he pulled himself up into the passenger's seat of the water tender ladder alongside me. We'd had the alert a matter of seconds earlier and were about to hit the road.

*Tree rescue at Montford Bridge*, read the initial message. We've got plenty of beautiful ancient forests, woods and copses in Shropshire. Trees stand like explosions of green all over the county. They stretch like fingers of life along our river banks and hedgerows. But there aren't too many in that particular corner of our world. Plus it was odd to hear John say one of my mates might be involved. I couldn't see why any of them would be climbing trees, wherever they were. We'd climbed a lot of trees as kids. We'd fallen out of a few of them. But not any more.

'What mates?' I asked cautiously, because this sounded like a wind-up.

'Exactly. Windsor hasn't got any mates,' Dodger pitched in from the back row.

I made a mental note to whack him on the side of his head when we got off the engine. 'Which one of my many good mates are you talking about?' I asked John.

'Your gliding pals. One of them just hang-glided himself into a tree,' he said.

I winced. I'd been hang-gliding for some time. There was a club over on the Long Mynd and I'd follow the others running from the top by the Midland Gliding Club and stepping off into the sky. The ridge lift was both incredibly powerful there. The view of Shropshire, laid out in a jigsaw of fields, roofs, gardens and trees, all criss-crossed with streams and roads and hedgerows, was like nothing else you could ever see. I'd struggled like anything to describe it to friends and family – as well as to the lads at work. But it was almost impossible. Till you've been up there, suspended in that rush of cold air and at the mercy of the vagaries of winds and up-draughts, you can't quite imagine what our glorious county really looks like. You can't grasp how far you can see. You can't understand how you get to know your county from up high. If I did more hang-gliding – or if I took the next step and began microlighting – it might even help when we headed out into the middle of nowhere to find some distant farm or house. When we were lost on the ground, I could imagine myself in the skies and what I would be able to see from up there. That way we might have a better idea where each farm or homestead was located.

The other thing I could never quite get across was how peaceful it was up in the skies. Yes, the wind whistled past your ears. It was noisier than you'd think. But there was calmness, somehow, even amidst the roar of the wind. Throw in the out-of-body sensation you got when you rode a wave of air, the adrenaline that surged as you came into land, and it has to be one of the most exhilarating hobbies going.

I snapped out of my reverie as I turned the engine onto the Forton road towards an old wartime airfield. The thought that someone – possibly someone I knew – could get in trouble and end up smashing into a tree was sobering. You'd hit it like a

train. You'd have, what, a pair of goggles, a helmet and gloves
to protect you. It didn't bear thinking about.

'Poor sod,' I said as I hit the accelerator and we gained speed
and momentum. We passed through a narrow lane where the
trees curved above us and connected. In summer, when the
leaves were full, it must have resembled a green tunnel. In the
autumn it was like a rich brown rabbit hole. Out the other
side we headed towards the airfield. I breathed in deeply as I
took my eye off the road momentarily and looked out over the
fields. They didn't roll so much, over here. From the height of
the cab you could see for miles. My eyes traced the path of a
well-worn bridleway that disappeared into the far distance. It
was glorious. The most beautiful county, I believed.

'Right, nearly there. I still can't quite get my head around
what's happened here. I still think Jeremy Beadle is going to
jump out,' I said, pulling us round the final corner. Ahead,
on the left, I saw a wooden sign proclaiming Montford Bridge
Parachute Club. I'd never even known it existed. I should find
out more, I thought, perhaps I'd join up one day, if I ever got
bored of hang-gliding.

'It's not Jeremy Beadle. But he looks like a bit of a joker,'
Dodger said drily as I slowed the engine. For once Dodger was
being kind. The guy looked like an idiot.

He was your classic hippy-dippy type, probably in his
mid-twenties. It was a cold November day but he was wearing open-toed leather sandals. It was 1987 but he was wearing
a multicoloured woollen sweater from the Seventies. Instead
of jeans he was wearing a baggy and faded flight suit. As I
looked closer, he appeared to have a couple of coloured beads
tied in one side of his long, shaggy hair. He had a sort of knit-
ted bag over his shoulder and army-green fingerless gloves on
his hands. I'm sure he was a lovely guy, but at first glance he

seemed a bit of a prat. I didn't really want the lads to think he was one of my pals. And I was even more determined to distance myself from him when he opened his mouth.

'Hey, guys, good to see you at last. You took your time, though, didn't you? I thought you'd got lost or given up. I thought I'd have to call another Fire Brigade and see if the boys from Wales could do a better job.'

A word to the wise. That's not the kind of greeting that will help you make friends and influence people when the Fire Brigade turns up. Another word to the wise. Don't follow it up with this: 'Can I cadge a lift, man? I'll show you where we're going.' Especially if you're climbing on to the running board as you ask the question.

Unable to shake him off – literally or figuratively – I put the engine in gear. 'We're heading down there,' he said, pointing down the full length of a wide tarmac runway. Then he said something else that piqued our interest and distracted us from what a plonker he was. 'She's over there in the far corner,' he told us. It was the word 'she' that did it. That was a good word. We liked rescuing women. All firemen do.

'What's this all about? We were told it was a hang-gliding accident,' I began as all sixteen tonnes of us dug into the wet, muddy grass on the edge of the runway.

'No, we don't do hang-gliding. Are you crazy, man? We're a parachute club. She was parachuting. Her name's Vanessa. It was her first jump.'

'What happened?'

'Well, when we got up there, she wasn't keen on jumping out. Funny how often that happens.'

'Did you push her?' Dodger asked.

Our hippy friend looked horrified. 'We're a very reputable flying club. We'd never push someone out,' he began.

I only hoped he didn't hear Martin in the back saying: 'I'd push you out, pal' in a whisper that was anything but quiet.

Our new friend, fortunately, was too keen on the sound of his own voice. He carried on talking regardless. 'She couldn't do it first time, but we just did a fly around and tried to talk her into it. She knew the drill. She'd done all the training. She had her wobble. Lots of people do. It's natural. But she's a big, brave girl. I knew she'd do it in the end. So when we got back around, she was ready. So she did it, brave girl. She jumped.'

'Was it a static line?' I asked. 'One thousand, two thousand, three thousand, check canopy?' I asked, showing off. The other lads looked genuinely surprised. Young hippy man did, I'm pleased to say, look a little bit impressed as well.

'That's right. You must be a fellow flier. Marvellous to know you, man. And that's exactly what Vanessa was trained to say and do.'

'But she didn't?'

'No. She jumped, and she says she kept her eyes tight shut. The only thing she said was a prayer.'

'So what happened?'

'She came down any old how. She kept her arms clenched across her chest all the way down. She went in whatever direction the wind took her.' We were almost at the end of the runway at this point. A few hundred yards further on was the only small copse of trees in the vicinity. It was the only one for quite some distance. 'It was blindingly obvious that she was heading right towards the trees. We went crazy trying to alert her. Our instructor on the ground was screaming at her through the walkie-talkie strapped to her chest. We were screaming from the plane – not that anyone could have heard us from there. Everyone was screaming. We were shouting our heads off to get her to do some steering. It worked, but only at the very, very end. She came out of her stupor. She woke up fast. She saw where she was and where she was going. It was her turn to scream, poor love. She grabbed the toggles at last and steered to the left. She did everything she could to avoid the impact. But it was too late. She hit the top of the tree. And that's where she's stayed.'

I stopped us, pulled on the brake and we all jumped to the ground. The little clump of trees ahead of us was incredibly isolated. Steering into them wouldn't have been that easy. The odds of finding them were long. It was sod's law that Vanessa had done so by accident.

'Vanessa, it's me! The cavalry are here!' our friend shouted up at her.

'I'm stuck!' her voice came down.

'Thanks for that information,' Martin whispered, once again a little too loud. Then he relented and shouted up. 'We'll get you down, miss. Are you injured?'

'No, I'm fine. It's just my pride that's hurt. I've maybe got a few scratches. I think I dislodged a bird's nest with my head.'

'Well, we don't need to worry about that.'

We approached and encircled the copse – which was actually bigger than it had first appeared. Vanessa's pale yellow parachute was laid out over the top of the tallest tree, bang in the middle. She was hanging in her harness a few yards below it and at least twelve feet away from the nearest tree trunk. She was around thirty feet above the ground. And she was swaying, ever so slightly, in the autumn breeze.

'Tricky, tricky,' John said as we stood back by the fire engine.

You couldn't easily get to any of the dozen or so trees in the middle of the copse. Every inch of ground round their trunks was covered in dense, yard-high and heavily overgrown briars, saplings, bramble bushes and other spikey hazards. Together they created a natural barrier like the one round Sleeping Beauty's castle.

'Have you not got a ladder?' our flying friend asked, helpfully.

We bit our lips in unison. It was already clear that the issue wasn't our lack or otherwise of a ladder. It was the question of where to put it. With Vanessa suspended in mid-air, and so far from the nearest trunk, the problem was working out how we could reach her. In my experience, it's always nice to have something to lean a ladder against. That day there was nothing.

Suddenly Caddie's voice came into my head. 'Let's give it a couple of coats of looking at,' he'd been wont to say at unusual incidents like this. So we did just that. We looked at it from as many angles as we could. Then we came up with a plan.

'Get the 13.5,' John instructed. This was our longest ladder, around 5 metres at its shortest and 13.5 metres when extended, hence the name. It was also around a metre wide and as heavy as it looked.

'Get it in there,' he said, nodding his head towards the copse.

A low groan came from the rest of us. Carrying that ladder was no fun on the nice flat training ground, where we tended to use it the most. Carrying it through the thorn bushes towards Sleeping Beauty was going to be a whole different ball game. But it didn't look as if we had a choice. Martin, Ben and I hacked away at the vegetation to clear a path. The thorns on the brambles were everywhere and they got everywhere. The ground under our feet was equally hazardous. They could have filmed *Watership Down* in that copse, for all the rabbit holes we stumbled over and got our feet trapped in. But with a fair damsel in distress looking down on our every move, no one wanted to be the first to complain or, worse, to cry out.

'Bloody hell, I'm sweating like a pig,' Martin said at one point. We all were. It might have been a cold and breezy autumn day, but when you're in fireman's kit and you're trying to stamp a path through undergrowth like that, you make a lot of heat. Especially when you're carrying a ladder.

'I'm so grateful. I'm so sorry to have caused all this trouble. I do feel very foolish,' Vanessa shouted down. She was probably in her mid-twenties and we'd all noticed the lovely chestnut hair spilling out from under her helmet. We'd all noticed how pretty she was as well. She had soft pale skin and lovely eyes. So, of course, none of this was too much trouble. Especially as in the appeal stakes she was already a million miles ahead of her friend in the silly sweater and sillier sandals.

'Lift the ladder up a bit, man, and you'll be fine,' he shouted helpfully.

'Wind your neck in and you'll be fine,' Martin echoed back.

A last few particularly nasty thorn bushes later and we were finally close to where we needed to be. It was time to get inventive. 'Right, let's tie those lines on,' commanded John, from a safe distance. We'd worked out our plan when we'd first got the ladder off the engine. With no tree to lean the ladder on we had decided to take the only other option. We were going to lean it on thin air.

Martin secured a line to the top right-hand side of the ladder. I did the same to the left. We then got ourselves ready, stepped back together and pulled it upright. Stage one complete, we extended it upwards so it aligned itself alongside the floating Vanessa. Then, thorns, briars and brambles all around, we tied off the ropes on the nearest, strongest tree trunks we could find.

'Secure,' I yelled from the left.

'Secure,' Martin confirmed from the right.

'That's incredible. That's so cool, man, so clever,' said our hippy pal, redeeming himself a little by being so impressed with our handiwork and improvisation.

'Thank you so much!' added Vanessa. Though she was somewhat premature, as we'd not actually got her down yet.

'Right, stand aside, men,' said our officer in charge and nemesis, John. He had already said he intended to pull rank and be the one to actually carry out the rescue. I'm not so sure he'd have done the same if it had been a hefty bloke rather than a beautiful woman suspended in mid-air, but there you go. He tested the ladder, looked all around, puffed out his chest and headed up into space. I smiled as I watched him go. From a short distance away, if you'd stood at an angle that hid the two ropes, it would have looked as if he was climbing some magically suspended stairway to heaven. And now I'd had that thought, the song wouldn't leave my head.

'Now, Vanessa, I'm going to reach out for you,' John was saying some thirty feet above us.

'Thank you! Thank you so much!' she said again.

'I'm going to pull you towards me.' We were all looking up intently. She seemed secure in the harness. She'd lasted this long. Surely she wouldn't slip free when the end was in sight?

She didn't, which was just as well as we don't carry the kind of hand-held trampoline thing I seem to remember comedy firemen having in the circus.

'I've got you,' John said confidently. He swung her right up against the ladder. She was whimpering, ever so quietly – and as she'd been dragged through space towards a forty-four foot ladder that appeared to be suspended in mid air she had good reason to do so. John muttered a stream of confident reassurances as he tackled the harness straps and freed his new passenger.

'Are you sure I won't fall?' she asked as the last of the straps was unfastened. 'I quite liked being attached to the parachute, now I think about it.'

'You're going to be fine,' John said reassuringly. He got her in position, securely standing in front of him on the ladder, and then it was time for the short descent. 'It's not far and we'll take it slowly, one rung at a time.'

Our hippy friend continued to redeem himself by giving a loud burst of applause when Vanessa was finally delivered on to the terra firma. 'Well done! Well done everyone! Marvellous stuff! Three cheers for the marvellous Shropshire Fire Brigade!' he shouted.

Vanessa, meanwhile, gave John an excited hug, turned to thank the rest of us, stumbled on a tree root and fell face first into a bramble bush. To her eternal credit she didn't miss a beat or stop smiling. If she thanked us once she thanked us a hundred times. In fact she was so grateful and so charming that once we'd untied and re-stowed the ladder we gave her a lift back to the club house where her eventful day had begun. Her friend, despite redeeming himself with his three cheers, had to walk.

Before we departed we asked her what time she'd first got into the plane. She told us, looking a little confused because understandably she didn't know why this might matter. 'And do you know what time you jumped?'

'I've no idea.'

'Do you know?' we asked our friend in the sandals.

'The first jumper went out at two thirty and we time these things quite carefully so she must have jumped at two thirty-five,' he said.

'Well, I looked at my watch when John got her off the bottom rung of that ladder,' said Pete. 'So her parachute jump took exactly fifty-seven minutes. That must be a record. We should call the *Guinness Book of Records* and get good old Norris McWhirter over here to give her a certificate.'

## 20

# Kids on a Cliff

John shot me a quick look the moment the tannoy went quiet. 'This looks like your big day, Windsor. Time to join your pals from the climbing course and see if you can do it all for real.'

I didn't need to be told twice. A cyclist had called us from a small hotel in the middle of nowhere. He'd seen three youths trapped at the Forest Glen, a cliff some 110 feet high on the edge of the Wrekin. Now you shouldn't ever pre-judge people in this job – or in life, come to that. But my gut instinct wasn't that these were intelligent mountaineers who'd got into difficulties despite having the best kit and training at their disposal. No, I had a feeling that these would be our current scourge – idiots who'd climbed the cliff armed with spray cans of paint to try to add their own splash of graffiti to the mix that was already there.

And so they were.

In total six of us who'd been on the climbing course – from a variety of stations and watches – regrouped at the Wrekin. It was the first time we'd seen each other since the training had ended. The first time we'd done any of this in anger. And you could tell straight away that we were excited as anything.

I'd headed out in the station Land Rover in my new cliff-rescue kit – basically a blue tracksuit and a blue fleece. All the other kit and equipment was in the back behind me. We had a pre-planned routine to rendezvous at the scene of the rescue. Everyone got there in a variety of vehicles, but someone would always be nominated to bring the kit in the Land Rover. Today, that was my job. The journey was great – not least because I was on my own, so I didn't have to put up with anyone's elbow in my face, anyone's smelly feet in the air and everyone's ridiculous banter taking up the whole trip. Instead I sang songs at the top of my voice wearing a great cheesy grin on my face.

The countryside got more and more beautiful with each song I murdered. The Wrekin is a unique and unmistakable part of our world out here. It stands some 1,350 feet high and it's hundreds of millions of years old. There's an Iron Age fort near the top and other archaeological and geological sites all over. It's littered with fault lines and the cut of old tin and lead mines. Local legend has it that it wasn't formed by volcanic activity, continental shift or anything else. Legend says it was created by an angry giant who had a grudge against dear old Shrewsbury. Here's what is said to have happened.

Our giant woke up one day and decided to destroy Shrewsbury once and for all. He dug up a huge clump of rock and earth and put it into an enormous wheelbarrow. Then he headed towards the town, planning to dump the rocks in the Severn and cause a terrible flood. But he got tired on the way, and he was duped by a cobbler who persuaded him that Shrewsbury was miles away – so the clump of earth got dropped there, instead, and the giant headed home to take a nice rest and dream up some other wild scheme. And the barrow of earth? It's the Wrekin, so they say.

Back in the real world, I slapped a lot of backs and shook a lot of hands as the six of us from the training group had a mini-reunion. Everyone was well up for the challenge.

And up ahead the three lads we were there to rescue were attracting a fair bit of attention – not much of it sympathetic. The cliff rises above and behind a gravel car park where hikers, bikers, walkers and climbers leave their vehicles. About half a dozen drivers were standing around, pointing and shouting at the kids some fifty feet above them. The lads were wearing dark jeans and coats. From a distance, as I had driven towards the Forest Glen, they had looked like shadows against the grey stone of the cliff. From the car park itself they looked like scared little idiots.

I decided to take the lead for a while. 'Right, this is the Fire Brigade, as you can probably see. Can you all hear me?' I yelled up from the base of the cliff. The kids were some way from each other. I'd expected them to be clumped together. Only one of the three had acknowledged us so far. The other two hadn't even moved.

'Are they all right?' I asked one of the hikers who said he'd been watching them for about twenty minutes. He shrugged. He didn't seem to care.

'Can you all hear me?' I shouted again. We needed a response. If any of them was unconscious we needed to know so we could prioritise him for the first rescue.

This time I got two shouts in reply. It wasn't enough. 'Can all three of you hear me? I want each of you to shout out your name so we know you're OK.'

They did it, in the end. And, in a faltering explanation shouted down with a mix of embarrassment, fear and bravado, we soon got a picture of what had happened. As I'd suspected, they were vandals rather than intelligent mountaineers. Fortunately for the rocks of Shropshire, one of them had stumbled before they'd done any damage. The trio had been a long way up when the biggest lad in the group tripped and fell about twelve feet before hitting a stone ledge with what had to have been a heck of a thump. He had fallen a whole lot further before landing on another, wider ledge. He had tried to get up at this point, only to realise that he'd broken his lower leg.

The other two had then learned one of the surprising lessons of climbing: going up can be a hell of a lot easier than climbing down. I imagine they'd not realised how high they were when they were having fun heading up to their prime position in the middle of the cliff. You don't really notice the distance you travel when you are always looking up for the next hand hold. It's a different matter when you look down for a good foothold. That's when you lose your head – and sometimes your balance.

One of the other two had slipped as he tried to get to his mate or to get back down to safety himself. He'd scrambled sideways, fallen again and ended up on a ledge of his own. At that point he'd promptly frozen with fear. The third of them stuck exactly where he'd been. He'd frozen even more completely. He was the quiet one who didn't want to open his mouth, let alone his eyes.

'You with the black woollen hat on. Are you sure you're not hurt in any way?' I shouted at him one last time. In this job it's the quiet ones we have to watch, in anything from road accidents to, well, cliff rescues. The ones who are screaming and shouting and getting all dramatic are usually OK. It tends to be the ones who say nothing who turn out to have the life-threatening injuries. They're in shut-down mode. And they're in danger.

'I'm fine. Just get me the eff off this cliff,' he shouted in the end. It wasn't fighting talk. All the bravado he or his gang possessed was gone by that point. A cold wind was blowing and there was rain in the air. The lads were pussycats now. I only hoped they had nine lives.

'There's nothing like jumping in at the deep end. In training we rescued one person at a time. And the first time we're doing it for real, there's three of the buggers,' said Vincent as we had a conflab about the situation.

'Well, we've got two basic options—' said Sam.

'Three, if we include leaving the buggers up there to think about the implications of criminal damage,' interrupted Vincent.

'If only,' said Sam. Then we all got serious. The temperature was falling fast as daylight faded away. The rain had held off, but the clouds ahead were as grey and threatening as ever. We needed to act while the rocks, and the kids, were dry. 'Option one is to climb up to them, secure a strong belay point in the rock above them and lower them down to safety. We can do it one at a time, or a couple of us can go at the same time then go back for the last of them.'

We looked up at the cliff to consider how hard or easy that job would be. 'The second option is to set up an anchor point at the top of the cliff, lower ourselves down to each casualty in turn, strap them to us and then continue down to the bottom, taking them with us.'

'That's the one I would go for,' I said as we considered it all. Heading down from above was almost always the safest option, as it didn't require us to climb up the cliff and to find a belay point that was firm enough to carry both our weights.

'There are some decent trees up top. They'll be pretty bomb-proof as anchor points,' Gareth said to the rest of the gang as we carried on weighing up the pros and cons. We'd done some training on this cliff in the past, so we knew the lie of the land.

'Then that's what we do. Let's get the kit and get up there,' said Vincent.

The first four of us got all the kit we needed on our backs

and round our waists and headed up to the top of the cliff. The other two were left in the car park to reassure the lads from below, to share some dry comments with the hikers, and to act as support to us once we began our descent.

It was a good five minutes before we got to the trees up top. It was cold, but you still sweat on climbs like that. Especially when you're as loaded down as a pack mule. We rigged up two sets of descending lines on two separate anchor points.

'You and me, right?' I said to Miles, who was next to me. We'd worked on a few climbs and cave trips as buddies on the course so we knew and trusted each other. He nodded and we set about checking our kit. We had a mass of stuff, including karabiners, slings, chocks and rocks in case we needed to make a fresh anchor point halfway down. We also had rescue slings, similar to the ones you see in air–sea rescues with helicopters.

Then we got ready for the off. We didn't do the Hollywood thing of throwing a rope over the cliff edge – where you run the risk of whacking the person you're trying to rescue over the head and knocking him to his doom. Instead we kept the bulk of our lines in the bags attached to our climbing belts. We made sure we were fully attached to the lines, gave the thumbs up and then headed backwards over the edge of the cliff. I've got to say I felt a bit like James Bond – Sean Connery, though, not Roger Moore.

'Here we go. See you at the bottom! Best of British to you, chum!' Miles called out.

'And to you, mate. Last one down buys drinks.'

The sun was sinking even lower in the sky as foot by foot we lowered ourselves. We were a little way away from the lads we were aiming for. We didn't want to be too close in case we dislodged any rocks on the way down and did them an injury.

'Right, pal, I'm here, I'm going to make sure your friend is safe then I'll come back and get you down to safety,' I told the first guy when I got into his line of sight. His eyes were closed tight. He was squeezing them the way scared little kids do when *Doctor Who* is on.

'My leg hurts. I think I've broken it,' he said weakly.

I glanced down towards the car park where something new was carving through the gravel. 'OK, an ambulance has arrived so you'll get looked after as soon as we get you down. Stay still just a few minutes more then it'll all be over.'

I moved my attention to the other guy near me. 'Mate, I'm going to secure you to where you are before helping your pal,' I told him.

'But you've got to get me down first,' he said.

'We think your friend has broken his leg. We'll get him down first, then we'll come for you.'

'I don't care about his effing leg. Get me down. I need to get down now.'

I was close enough to see the fire in the guy's eyes. I could practically smell the fear on his breath. And I had to make a decision. You don't want someone on the edge of a cliff who's on the verge of panic. If he was so crippled with fear he might do something stupid then I would have no choice but to abandon his injured friend and take him down first. And that didn't seem right.

'Hold on where you are. I'm putting this sling round your chest,' I said, removing the equipment from my bag and getting it in place. I then lodged a chock – a metal wedge that resembles a large nut on a short length of line – into a crack in the rock beside him. With the sling attached to that, he could stay safe till we got back to him. If he let us, that is.

'You can't effing leave me here!' he shouted.

'You're safe. We're going to help your friend now.'

'Screw him. Get me off this effing cliff.'

'Mate, I've broken my leg. I'm in agony. I need help,' the friend – or probably former friend – shouted out.

'That's your effing problem. This whole thing was your effing idea. I'm getting down off here and I'm getting down now.'

'Enough!' I yelled as Miles shouted the same from the other side of the cliff. We both knew we had to defuse this situation. You can't have a fight halfway up a cliff face. 'Look,' I told the guy I was alongside, as clearly and authoritatively as I could. 'Your mate is going to be taken down the cliff first. You are totally safe where you are. I want you to stay still and wait. Do you understand me?'

'Yeah but I don't see why—'

'Do you understand me?'

'Yes.'

'Then wait, don't move, and shut up.'

I made it back to the lad with the broken leg just as Miles reached the last of the trio. We got them attached to us in rescue slings before pushing back and edging down the rock face to the car park. Broken-leg boy was crying out so loud at times I had to tell him to shut up as well. I couldn't hear myself think, let alone hear any warnings from above, below or from Miles. And all he had was a suspected broken leg, for Pete's sake. These had to be the most pathetic vandals in the county.

'Nearly there, a few feet more,' I muttered. Then I felt the more level ground of the car park edge beneath my feet. Miles and I had made it at almost exactly the same time.

I lowered him the final foot just as the ambulance guys got to us. They had their stretcher with them and they put him on it and said nice reassuring things as they carried him to the ambulance. That's a bit excessive, I thought to myself as I watched them go. I'd have made him hop there.

'You want to go back up or shall I?' Miles asked when his equally sullen victim had been freed.

'I'll do it, if you don't mind?' I said. 'I love doing this.'

So off I went. I rejoined the other two crew at the top of the cliff then did the whole job again. I really enjoyed the task. There was something about cliff work that felt incredibly energising. I guess you either have a head for heights or you don't. We've all got different strengths. I might suffer from crippling travel sickness, but at least I could climb. Not that my new friend on the ledge shared my enthusiasm.

'Where are you? Why aren't you here? I'm still here! Where are you?' he kept shouting as I began my final descent.

'I'm coming. Stay still,' I yelled down at him.

'I effing hate this,' he muttered.

'Then don't climb cliffs in the first place,' I muttered back at him under my breath.

'You should have taken me down first,' were the first words he said when I pulled myself alongside him.

'Your mate's probably got a broken leg,' I pointed out, for what felt like the tenth time.

'I don't give a monkey's,' he said sulkily. 'It was his idea to come up here. You should have rescued me first.'

Trying not to smile, I attached him to my harness and then disconnected him from the chock arrangement.

'Don't drop me,' he cried out, a baby again, as I pushed back and began to bounce us down the cliff. This time I don't think I managed to hide the smile.

'Stay still,' I said as we got to the final ten or twelve feet of the mini-descent.

'I want to get off.'

'Well, you can't.'

Did I extend the time it took to go down those last few jumps, simply to prolong his agony and teach him a lesson? I couldn't possibly comment. But in the end we were on solid, flat ground and I have to say I was only too happy to unclip the guy's harness and let him break free from me. He shuffled over, joined his mate who was standing near the back of the ambulance. They held a huddled conference and it looked for a while as if the first of them was trying to think of the right words to say to us. 'Thank you,' might have been a good start. 'Sorry,' would have been a good follow-up. The words eluded them both. The pair of them just stood and stared at their boots. Then they got ready for the next set of consequences of what they'd done. Another car was pulling into the car park. A police car.

'Hello, Norman, good to see you. Let me introduce you to our new pals,' I said as he approached. I was glad it was Norman. He didn't do the whole softly, softly thing. He thought criminals were criminals, not misunderstood victims of circumstance. He certainly wouldn't have got that stretcher out.

I was grinning even more broadly as I left them all to it and headed back to the bottom of the cliff. The others had untied the lines and cleared up the mini-camp of kit we'd built up at the top, and were making their way down.

'Not exactly satisfied customers, are they?' Vincent said as we headed back to our vehicles.

'You could hear all that, could you?' I asked.

'Every word. "Don't drop me! I want to get off!"' he mimicked. 'What a bunch of babies.'

'"Don't save my mate, save me!"' Sam followed up.

'Let's hope they're getting a good talking to. Old Norman's been reading the riot act to them for some time,' Vincent said as we watched the pair sitting in the back of the police car for their not-so-friendly chat.

One of the last things I saw as we got ready to leave was a forgotten can of black spray paint that must have dropped out of a pocket and bounced and rolled its way down the slope. It had ended up a fair distance across the car park. For some reason I was determined not to leave it there. Shropshire is one of the most beautiful places on earth. I didn't want anyone else being tempted to destroy a single rock. Plus I knew we could find some use for it in our workshop. After all, Martin's next set of wrought-iron gates wouldn't paint themselves.

## 21

# Nicholas Does It Again

~

Five words were all it took. The rest of Red Watch were out on a shout when I got back to the station after the cliff rescue. They would be relieved by Green Watch at the scene of the shout when the night shift clocked on at six. I twiddled my thumbs at the station as I waited for the end of the shift. Eventually 6 a.m. came and I headed home . . . then said the usual five words at the start of our next shift:

'So, what did I miss?'

The whole watch fell about laughing.

'Blimey, it must have been good. It was a house fire, wasn't it? How could that be so funny? What the heck happened?' I looked around all the faces as I asked the questions. Charlie, Woody, Dodger and the other youngsters were obviously enjoying the joke, whatever it was. Arfer, Martin, Pete and the rest of the old-timers were laughing equally loud. John and Joe were in on it too. Only one man had a different expression on his face. At first he was gazing skyward, as if he wanted the ground to swallow him up. Then he sat down, put his head in his hands and shook it slowly from side to side.

I started to laugh myself at the sight.

'Nicholas, mate, what have you done now?' I asked.

His head stayed firmly in his hands.

'It was over in Radbrook Green . . . wasn't it? A kitchen fire? A chimney fire? What was it? Were there persons reported? What the hell happened?'

'The fire was in the garage,' Woody began, putting me out of my misery, but doing nothing to ease the tortured look on Nicholas's face. 'It was one of those semi-detached places with a bedroom over the garage. The dad had been having a crafty fag in the garage where he hoped his wife wouldn't see. She'd come in, all of a sudden, so he'd thrown it away without stubbing it out properly.'

'And what do most of us have in garages? Junk, cardboard boxes, oil canisters, tins of thinners, meths, camping gas cylinders, old petrol cans, matches, candles, tumble driers all full of bone-dry fluff – everything you need for a very fierce fire. The backin' idiot,' interrupted Arfer.

'Well, either way, the fire looked set to spread. There was a lot of confusion among the neighbours with no one sure who was where and what was going on. Not one of them spoke a sensible sentence the whole time we were there.'

'But there were persons reported, so it was serious,' said Charlie. I flashed a glance at him. It was rare for him to be the voice of reason in any conversation. 'The neighbours said two girls were missing. Aged five and seven.'

'Not good,' I said, trying to work out what could possibly have happened. 'Who was on BA duty?'

'I was one of them,' said Joe drily.

'And the other?' I asked. No one spoke. But Nicholas took one of his hands away from his face and held it up. It was almost a sign of surrender. I felt genuinely sorry for him. But I laughed as well. What the hell had he done?

'We got in there and we did the business. To be fair to young Nicholas, visibility was bad. The smoke was thick and all the windows had been shut, so it had been building up the whole time.'

'It was noisy as well. There was a lot of noise. It's easy to miss things,' Nicholas added. He was sitting upright now, wearing the rueful, half-embarrassed smile that we'd come to know so well.

'And you did miss something, didn't you, lad?' prompted Joe.

'Just a bit,' he admitted.

'He missed the fact that the two girls had been found safe and well. They were at their best pal's house across the road. They were watching the action from her bedroom window. Their mum and dad were downstairs. Everyone was present and accounted for. Everyone knew that. Everyone except for young Nicholas.'

'So I was searching like a mad man. I've still not done that many persons reported shouts, remember? I was fizzing with excitement, determined to find those kids. It was my big moment. I was going to prove myself. I was going to save them. No one was going to die when I was in that fire.'

Joe took up the story. The younger girl's bedroom was the one above the garage, and it had taken a bit of a hit from the fire. He and Nicholas had followed procedure when they got to it. They had moved around the small room from different angles. Joe had gone to the left and hugged the wall, feeling every surface along the way, while Nicholas had gone to the right. The plan is always to meet in the middle, having covered all the possible space.

What we also learn in training is to be alert in situations like that. People are rightly terrified in fires. They've not been trained, the way we have. So they do things we'd never do. That includes hiding in unusual or unlikely places – and leaping out at us when we least expect it.

Often if they can't get out through windows or doors, people trapped by fire climb under tables or creep into cupboards, trying to find shelter. It's a natural instinct. Sometimes, when we come into the room they are in, they jump out in front of us. Other times they wait. Maybe they can't believe it, or don't want to believe it in case it's not true. They're terrified that they're deluded. So it's only when we get right up to them, when they're absolutely sure that a real, living, breathing fireman is in the room, that they jump up. It scares the blinkin' heck out of us. They do it like bats out of hell sometimes. And if we're all kitted out, breathing apparatus on and gloved up, we can't sense things till they're on us. Like I say, it scares the heck out of us.

Anyway, the lesson is that you can never assume a room is empty simply because all is still. People might still be there. So you keep on looking. It's also true that you can't assume a room – or even a whole house – is empty just because you're told it is. Let's say it's a teenage girl's bedroom. Who knows whether that's the night the girl's boyfriend stayed over – and no one else knew. Who knows if she had a pal her parents didn't approve of across for a secret sleep-over. Or if any number of other people are there for any number of unlikely reasons.

With all that in his freshly trained mind Nicholas had been deadly serious in his search. And as he told the story – with an awful lot of interruptions – it appeared that he had found someone.

'I was at the edge of the bed,' he said. 'It was small, a kid's bed. That made everything seem all the more real, somehow. I got my hands out. I ran the back of them along it to see what might be there. And you can't feel a damn thing properly in those gloves. You've all known that for years. I know it now.'

I shook my head, looking around at all the laughing faces. I had a horrible feeling I knew where this was going.

'I found someone,' Nicholas declared. 'I found one of the kids. I didn't know they were safe and sound on the other side of the street.'

'He yelled it out. He scooped them up. He carried them low. And he got them out of the house fast. I'll give him that, he did everything right. It was all by the book,' Joe said, still smiling.

'I talked to the kid all the way across the landing and down the stairs. I didn't suppose she could hear a word through all the BA kit. But I wanted her to know she was safe. I told her I was a fireman. I said everything was going to be OK. I kept her wrapped up in the duvet for protection. I had her in my arms and I held her close. We'd got a bit of ventilation going, but the smoke was still thick. It was hard as hell to see. Still, we got across the hall and out the front door.'

'What happened then?'

'I yelled for first aid. I yelled again and again. I'd picked up the pace and was running down the front path to get some fresh air for the girl and get her to the ambulance quickly. And then,' Nicholas said, turning his head to one side and exhaling loudly, 'And then I started to realise something was wrong.'

'He laid the little lady on the ground,' said Joe. 'He was still shouting for first aid. He said we needed to carry on the search for the second kid. He started to wipe the soot and dirt off his face mask so he could see more clearly.'

'I was getting ready to give the kid mouth to mouth,' said Nicholas. 'If no one else was going to help then I was going to do it myself.'

'And what happened next?'

'Every other bugger on the watch started to laugh. That's what happened.'

'Why?'

'Because wrapped up in the duvet and on the ground in front of me was a three-foot-tall teddy bear. The kind you win at a coconut shy at a fair,' Nicholas said, to another roar of laughter from the rest of the gang.

'There's a stuffed giraffe over in Telford that's trapped on a top bunk. Maybe you could use the long ladder to rescue that one day,' Woody said as Nicholas made some impressively clear hand gestures to the room.

'And some kids in Telford went to Sea World on their summer holidays. They've got a stuffed killer whale. Can you give it mouth to mouth next time we go east on a shout?'

The jokes went on for the rest of the shift. They'd probably have gone on for a lot longer, but Nicholas turned out to be lucky. Someone else did something even more ridiculous.

'You had to see it to blinkin' believe it. It was a hundred to one shot. More than that. It was once in a lifetime,' Pete told us from behind the bar at the start of our next night shift. All was quiet and we were hunkering down for the duration. A cold front had hit earlier in the week and things were getting icy. Cold weather normally keeps us busy – all sorts of fires are lit in houses and farms, while all sorts of crazy accidents can strike on the roads. But so far so good. We'd eaten a great dinner. Now we were having a laugh over a few drinks.

'It was the retained crew from Church Stretton. They were doing a combined drill with White Watch. Ray was in charge. He was really putting them through their paces. He'd got them using every bit of equipment in the yard. They did OK, by all accounts.'

'I don't believe that for a moment,' interrupted Martin, who didn't have the best opinion of our retained colleagues.

'Well, they didn't do anything wrong or break anything.

They got it all loaded back on to the appliances double quick. Anyway, Ray was playing sergeant major, doing the debrief, when there was a screech of brakes and an almighty crash. Of all places, someone had chosen the outside of the fire station to mow down an old guy as he crossed the road.'

'It was a woman driver,' Martin began, to groans and cat-calls from almost everyone. 'She'd knocked the guy flat as a pancake. She'd gone right into him and knocked him on to his back.'

'Did she kill him?' a bloodthirsty Dodger asked.

'He was all right, actually. He was in better shape than she was. One of his legs was trapped under the back wheel of the car, but he was conscious. She was hysterical, of course. She'd opened the car door after the crash, seen what she'd done and frozen. She was just sitting there, holding on to the steering wheel like there was no tomorrow, unhurt but in floods of tears.'

'She then got the fright of her life when all eighteen of the Church Stretton retained firemen thumped across the road towards her. Like a herd of uniformed rhinoceroses,' said Pete.

'I think it's rhinoceri,' said Charlie, not entirely convincingly.

'But if she got a fright it was nothing to the one Ray was about to get. He'd yelled out to have an ambulance called and for the station first-aid kit to be brought out. Then he went to deal with the guy under the rear wheel. The guy was laughing so hard you could've heard him halfway across town.'

'Why was he laughing? Shock?' I asked.

'Not quite. He was laughing because it was funny. Ray asked him if he could feel his leg. He said no. And he carried on laughing.'

'It had to be shock. It often makes people act strange.'

'Well, it was Ray who got the shock this time. The old guy

only went and stood up. He left his whole leg where it was, under the wheel.'

'Amputated? Sliced in two?' asked Dodger, agog.

'Not even close. Of all the people, in all the world, and in all the ways that woman could have run over someone, she'd hit a guy with a wooden leg! She'd actually driven over his wooden leg! He got a bit of bruise when he fell over on his backside, and some cuts and scratches on his hands. But apart from that, the only damage done was when he split his sides from laughing.'

## 22

# 'She's Behind You!'

$\infty$

The snows came down the week between Christmas and New Year. The whole county looked the like the Christmas cards on all our mantelpieces. It deadens the sound, puts a blanket – almost literally – over the countryside and moves everything on to super-slow time.

But beauty can be deadly. The roads can become treacherous. Whole corners of our county can be cut off. Fortunately, our farming communities are always ready for it. They keep enough food in their kitchens to see out at least a week of isolation. They have enough wood to stay warm and often have their own power generators as well. Most of the time families can sit tight for as long as it takes. Unless, let's say, one of them is about to have a baby.

The call came in shortly after eleven, when we were on an extended tea break in honour of the season. Charlie was smiling broadly after road-testing some new biscuits. 'A sort of oat crunch. They're a lot thicker than your average biscuit. Perfect for dunking, though you've got to check they don't break. A hundred times better than Rich Tea. We're going up in the world at last,' he was saying.

The rest of us were tucking into other seasonal fare. Maggie was having some time off with her family, but before leaving she had baked every watch a Christmas cake. A huge debate was going on about which of us had been given the biggest and best of them.

With a couple of good films due on the telly that afternoon we weren't best pleased to be called for an incident that sounded very minor. The initial call only mentioned a car broken down in the middle of nowhere. 'What's that got to do with us? Can't they get the AA?' Charlie moaned, crumbs falling from his face as he talked.

We were on the road by the time more information came in. The car wasn't broken down, it was stuck in a snowdrift. And the occupants weren't hardy farming folk who could trudge back home and return with a few shovels.

'A pregnant woman on her way to hospital. That's one for you, Arfer,' said Joe as we moved through the snow-less streets of Shrewsbury.

'I'm keeping my head well down. I might not even get out of the cab,' said Arfer, who we all knew was no big fan of babies or children.

'It certainly must be bad out there. It's not exactly a problem here,' Des said from the driver's seat. He was right. The main streets of Shrewsbury had been well tended. There was snow and ice aplenty, but it wouldn't have caused a normal car any problems, far less a hefty truck like ours. The snow did make the place look magical though. It matched the colours on the medieval half-timbered buildings. The faint street lights bounced off it. Over in the churchyard of St Chad's it probably made Ebenezer Scrooge's fake gravestone look even more authentic.

It did, of course, get worse as we headed across the county. Many of the side roads had barely been touched. A few tracks showed the odd farm vehicle had moved down them, but I'd not have wanted to be attempting them in a Mini Metro. The country lanes were worse. And more snow was falling as we headed south. Des drove well. Some of the hairpin bends we went round were tough going at the best of times. Sticking to those winding, sloping roads was no easy task. And as we left the last few villages and woods behind, things got even tougher. You're in snowdrift territory when the rolling hills and fields stretch out on either side of the road. The icy Shropshire winds had pushed the snow across the land – and dumped a heck of a lot of it in our path.

'Is that heater up as far as it'll go, Des?' Arfer asked from the rear seat.

I was leaning forward to try to see ahead of us. We had to be one of the few vehicles out there that morning. There looked to be only one relatively recent track in the road.

'And there's what made those tracks, but they're in desperate need of snow tyres, I reckon,' said Des. The tyre tracks I'd spotted ended just ahead, where a marooned ambulance was waiting for our arrival.

'Hello, lads, given up, have you?' Des asked as we jumped down to speak to the medics. Arfer, I noticed, was true to his word and was staying in the cab. It had been a good decision; the wind was vicious. It had icy claws. I pulled my fire tunic tight and looked enviously at Joe's thick, woolly hat.

'We've been skidding around like Bambi. We decided we'd call the heavy mob and see if you could sort things out for us.'

Des shrugged. 'Well, we'll not be going any further in this, seeing as you're slap bang in our way,' he said. 'Where's the car?'

The medic pointed up and around the roll of the hill. 'My colleague is with it. The woman's safe and warm inside, but she needs to get to hospital fast.'

We nodded and looked around. The lane was narrow and a few yards ahead it sank even further below the level of the fields. We could probably have got through the drifts, but we couldn't get past the ambulance, not when there might be hidden ditches on either side of us.

'It's a long way back to the nearest passing place,' said Joe. So it wasn't worth risking a reverse to get us ahead of the ambulance. No, we were at the end of our road. We'd have to do this one on foot. Four of us yomped up the hill to assess the situation. 'She's very, very pregnant, right enough,' was the considered opinion of the other medic at the scene.

'Can she walk?' Des asked.

'Can you engage your brain before speaking?' Joe replied. 'And for that stupid question you get the job of going back to our pals in the ambulance and getting a stretcher. You can carry it over here. And you can help carry it back to the ambulance when we've got our lady on it.'

Des did as he was told, kindly informing us when he returned just how much he was now sweating. We got the stretcher laid out, got the lady on it, wrapped up warm and secure, then tried to take giant steps back through the snow with it. I'd thought it might slide along the top, like a sledge. It didn't. It had to be lifted and lifted high.

'It's not me that's heavy, it's the baby,' the mum-to-be tried to joke early on as we struggled to manoeuvre her across the first part of the drift. Then she went quiet. Her face was tight and pinched. Her eyes seemed to go in on themselves. And she started to moan. So was this it? Was she going to give birth right here, in the snow?

'Nearly there, love. We've got a nice warm ambulance waiting for you just down the hill,' Joe said, a rare note of panic in his voice.

Arfer, who had finally deigned to leave the warmth of the cab and take a turn with the stretcher, had no cheery words of encouragement to offer. He'd taken over the end I'd been carrying. I felt myself smile as I sat back in the snow and tried to catch my breath. Arfer had to be the worst person to have at your side as you delivered a baby. It was mean of me, but I was secretly hoping her waters would break, just to see the look on his face.

'You didn't look as if you enjoyed that very much, my old friend,' Joe told him when the woman had been safely placed in the ambulance.

'Too many backin' kids in this world as it is. Can't believe we're helping add any more,' he muttered.

'I'm sure she'd have named it after you. There's always room for another Arfer, isn't there?'

'Backin' cheek,' was all he said in reply.

We never found out if the woman had a boy or girl. Though bearing in mind how much she had weighed on the stretcher, my money would have been on at least twins.

Kids were all around me the following week. I was playing Prince Charming in my drama group's latest panto, *Cinderella*. The dates had fallen badly for me. We were due on nights for the main performances – and after getting found out pulling a sickie last time, I'd booked these ones as annual leave. I'd not told many of the others. They'd be at the station, so none of them could come along and see it. Most of them knew I was in the show, but they didn't know what part I was playing. Though they soon found out – because once again I was going to end up with my photograph all over the local paper.

The photographer had got the entire cast together on

stage for the big photo. There were loads of us, standing, sitting, smiling like mad, and all in full costume and make-up. 'One more time, hold it right there and smile please!' he had said. And as the camera flash went off I gave the lads another classic mickey-taking opportunity. The picture went in the next issue of the paper. And despite the crowded photo, I was impossible to miss. I was there in the middle, six foot four and surrounded by some of the prettiest girls in Shrewsbury.

So what would the others say when I got to work?

What would they sing? I should have asked. I found out the moment I walked into the appliance room.

The whole of Green Watch was there. To a man they launched into Prince Charming – with full Adam and the Ants arm movements right off *Top of the Pops*.

That joke saw them through quite a long time, if I remember correctly. They kept singing it 'absent-mindedly' for weeks afterwards But at least none of them had found out about my other embarrassment. On my spiv job as a builder.

I'd been to give a quote for a job one evening. It was for replacing a section of the roof of a house over in the Copthorne area, one of the posher parts of town. I'd been saving up for a big ski trip, so the money was going to be handy. The job itself looked easy enough. The existing roof was in pretty good nick, truth be told. But some people have more money than sense – or maybe they've got money because they've got sense. Either way, not everyone waits till the rain comes through before they fix the roof.

Anyway, I returned in the daylight and climbed up on the roof, and was busy getting on with the job, muffled against the cold, when a neighbour approached.

'What are you doing?' he asked.

'The front crawl,' was what I wanted to say. What I actually said was: 'I'm replacing this section of roof for Mrs Pierce.'

The man looked at me and nodded slowly, the way Shropshire people do.

'Well, unfortunately you're on the wrong roof . . . you'll find Mrs Pierce lives next door but one,' he said.

I couldn't believe it, but the gates were the same, the front door was the same, and my first visit had been in the dark. I hadn't taken enough notice that morning to realise this wasn't the right house!

We passed the house – the right one – three days later on our next day shift. In theory we were on our way to fight another fire. In reality we were going to chase a big angry pig. Or, to be strictly accurate, a big angry pig was going to chase us.

The snows had melted and it was raining hard as we carved through some waterlogged country roads on our way to the address. Shrewsbury itself is always prone to flooding. With the River Severn and a host of other tributaries twisting all around, it's almost an island. It never took much to virtually cut it off.

'With a bit of luck this will have put the backin' thing out before we get there,' said Arfer, gazing morosely through the sheeting rain at the sodden fields beyond. 'I'd be very happy to stay in the cab in this weather.'

'And I'd be very happy to have a crew with a proper attitude. Just shows we can't all have what we want in this world,' said Joe.

The fire hadn't burned itself out when we got there. It was merrily working its way through a barn that could have doubled up as Santa's grotto. The place was jam-packed with junk. Boxes and crates and containers stood at least half a dozen deep and were piled high. There seemed to be a narrow access path between some of the stacks, but this petered out after a few yards. Just what this farmer stored, and why, was impossible to guess. And maybe he didn't even know himself.

'There's only a few things in there,' he said vaguely when Joe asked the question. As this was patently untrue, he was pressed. 'Well, it's built up a bit, over the years,' he admitted. 'If I don't need anything I put it in there for a while. Just in case. Just to see. But it's not a lot, really.'

'In places it's stacked taller than my house,' Joe pointed out.

The farmer looked into the smoke-filled interior, as if he was seeing it for the first time. He was a tall, craggy and con-fused-looking chap. He was probably in his early fifties, his clothes appeared to have been handed down from his dad, and he shrugged his shoulders an awful lot. He was doing so again. 'I put things there and sometimes I forget about them,' he admitted. 'Sometimes you do need things again. Fishing rods and things.'

We all looked into the barn now. Finding a fishing rod amidst all that junk would be like finding, I don't know, a needle in a haystack. 'There's nothing dangerous in there? No gas canisters, cylinders, machinery or fuel?'

For once the farmer seemed sure of his facts. 'It's just junk from the house. It's just, fishing rods and things,' he repeated, lapsing back into vagueness. We took him at his word. And we were already doing our best to help him out. Two of the others had been hosing down the outside of the barn so we could contain the blaze and stop it spreading – but after a second look around Joe decided we weren't doing enough.

'You've got a lot of livestock,' he said.

The farmer looked as vague as ever. It was as if he hadn't noticed. 'Few calves, few pigs,' he said.

'A few fishing rods,' I heard Woody mutter behind me.

'There's a lot of smoke. If the wind picks up, the fire could easily spread. I think we need to empty out these buildings to be on the safe side. The sooner we do it, the easier it will be,' said Joe. Famous last words.

The farmer went to open and close some gates on his nearest fields. Then we moved in on his animals. The first ones to tackle were the calves. They were great fun – a mass of big ears, wet noses, long gawky legs and surprised faces. They skipped and jumped around their pens as we opened the doors to move them to safety. And they didn't seem that keen on moving.

'I thought they'd make a run for it straight away,' said Woody. 'That's why we're always having to rescue the buggers. Because they run away and get in some kind of pickle.'

'Well, they're not running now,' I said.

We moved into the first pen to try to shoo its occupants towards the gate. One of them made an early bid for freedom. The others decided to pass. We waved our big firemans' arms around a bit, they kicked their big skinny legs a bit and it was clear we were at an impasse. 'It's more like herding cats than cattle,' said Woody. 'Time to get physical.' So we did. We made a grab for the calves and managed to manhandle them out into the yard and on to a safer place. We faced the same wet noses and surprised looks in all the other calving pens. Maybe it was the heavy rain, but the little fellows seemed quite happy where they were. And as usual it was only when weight of numbers came into play that they began to move of their own free will. When over half were already out of the barn the remainder decided to go with the flow. So with the calves all moved it was time to turn to the pigs.

'I'll see to them,' Arfer said, having deigned to get out of the warm, dry cab at last. Woody and I were only too happy to let him. The pigsty was a lot smaller and there were next to no inhabitants in it. Arfer was no fool, I thought. Or was he?

'Move it you, backin' little tykes,' he was saying as he tried to persuade a pair of piglets that they were better off in a wet, windy field. The 'backin' little tykes' decided not to follow his instruction. Instead they cowered in the corner of their sty. They were very appealing to look at. Their ears were almost as big as the ones on the calves. They were nicely hairy as well and seemed to have real personalities. 'Well, I asked nicely and you didn't listen,' Arfer said, reaching down and scooping the pair of them up. He kicked open the sty door and headed down the farmyard, a piglet under each arm.

And at that precise moment the little guys' mum appeared at the mouth of the sty. If the babies had been cute and docile then she was the exact opposite. She was big and mean and strong – and she was none too happy about this strange person walking off with two of her brood.

'Where the hell has she been hiding?' Woody muttered. 'I don't think Arfer knew she was there. Do we tell him?'

I caught the mischievous tone in his voice. I knew pigs, the way most of us did. They can see red worse than any bull in a field. They've got teeth and they can bite big chunks out of you. Mother pigs can be particularly dangerous when their babies are involved. 'I think we need to shut that pigsty door fast,' I said. But we were too late. The pig let out one of the most extraordinary roars I've ever heard and launched herself down the farmyard towards Arfer. She was like a small pink

Sherman tank. And she could probably do almost as much damage.

'Backin', backin' hell!' Arfer shouted, hearing the battle cry and swirling around in panic. He legged it to the far side of the yard then skidded to a halt. The farmer had just closed the gate to keep the calves in. And with a piglet under each arm, Arfer couldn't open it. I'm not sure I'll ever forget the look of panic on his face as he turned around. He was trapped. And the piglets' mum was gaining ground.

'Get them back in the sty!' Woody yelled, as Mum once more let out that horror-film battle cry. Arfer looked across the yard. You could almost sense his calculations. Could he make it? Could he get around the yard faster than the bat out of hell on his tail? He didn't have much choice. He shot off at a right angle, wrong-footing the angry mum, who wasn't fast enough to twist and turn straight away. He made a few useful yards. Then she skidded, stopped, steadied herself and prepared for a final assault. What, exactly, was this man doing to her babies now? How dare he! He had to be stopped.

'Open the door!' Arfer yelled as he took another sharp turn and aimed for his original starting point. We kicked the sty gate open and held it there with our boots. Arfer and his two pink little charges shot in. Seconds later their mum barrelled in as well – a seething mass of sweating resentment. Slamming the gate shut, Arfer then did a ballet-style leap over it – landing, on his backside, in a suspiciously muddy puddle in the yard.

'Never, never again am I going to offer to help when I don't have to,' he was muttering, as a piggy family reunion got underway back in the sty.

'Well, you're going to have to get those pigs out of there somehow,' said Joe, who'd been watching the show from the other side of the yard. 'We can't have them staying there. But I suggest you move them all together this time. And, Arfer, seeing as you're currently sitting in a pile of pig shit, you can be the one to play pied piper.'

# 23

# The Missing Chimney

∞

It was the last shift before I headed off on my big ski trip. The last shift before a two-week break I'd been looking forward to all year. And like so many other shouts, it would be full of surprises.

Our instructions at the start of the shout had been clear. We were on our way to tackle a chimney fire in a house situated close to the station on the outskirts of town. It had been called in by a neighbour in the middle of the afternoon. The odd news was that no one was reported to be inside the house – though of course that didn't mean no one was.

As the address in question wasn't far away, we had next to no time to pull our kit on in the back of the engines. I was on the appliance and had barely got ready by the time Ben turned into the small warren of residential streets that ran down towards the river. My mind was racing by that point. It always is for a chimney fire. You run through as many likely scenarios as you can. You check and double-check your kit. You try to prepare for anything.

That day, though, it looked as if we could have carried on with our volleyball game back at the station. The residential street we pulled on to was quiet. Ben counted up the house numbers till we got to the one in question. We jumped out

247

at number 19, where there was no sign of a fire. No sign of a chimney, either, as it happened. Interesting.

'False Alarm Malicious? Toe-rags with nothing better to do?' Pete hazarded, looking at the windows of the houses opposite to see if any guilty kids were watching. We headed through the garden gate to the rear of the house to give it the once-over from there. Still nothing. No flames, no smoke, no noise and no people.

We'd no sooner returned to the street than an oddly dressed elderly man came huffing and puffing around the corner. He was wearing what appeared to be a long tweed cape. His shoes were shiny black leather and pointed. To top it all, he had white hair and a wild white beard. He bore a striking resemblance to a wizard. A lean greyhound in a tatty tartan coat was straining at the leash ahead of him.

'Sir! Sir!' the man was shouting between wheezes and gasps for air.

'Looks like someone's mad old dad has turned up,' Charlie whispered wickedly as the old guy got closer.

'Can I help you, sir?' Joe asked, stepping forward as the wannabe wizard leaned on a lamp post to try to catch his breath. The dog jumped up to try to lick Joe, this huge, blue-suited stranger, to death. He also began to bark – not with aggression but with sheer, unadulterated joy. His thin grey tail was wagging like a helicopter rotor blade. His whole back end was wagging, truth be told. I'm not sure any of us would have been surprised if he hadn't defied the laws of physics and taken off.

'One second,' the man said, wiping his hand over his face and closing his eyes for a moment. In my head I did a quick recap of my first-aid training, in case I needed it.

'Take your time,' said Joe, clearly as worried as I was about the state of the old guy's heart.

The wizard nodded thankfully, took another gulp of air, then let rip. 'It's number 119, right round the bend where I've come from. The fire's at number 119 not number 19. I don't live on this street, I can't see so well any more and I read the number wrong and I'm very, very sorry,' he said in a torrent of words.

'It was you who called the Fire Brigade?' Joe asked.

'Yes, it was me.'

'And there's no one at home in the house in question?'

'No, it's empty. I banged on the door, then on all the neighbours' doors to raise the alarm when I saw the smoke, but no one was home anywhere. In the end I had to go all the way down to the river where there's a phone box by the garage. I went back to the house to wait outside and see if I could help. I saw you drive past at the end of the street. That's when I realised I'd given the wrong number. It's at number 119, I'm so very sorry. There's even more smoke now and it's looking really bad. Can you come?'

As if we'd say no.

'Is it far?'

'Two hundred yards. Maybe less?' he suggested.

'Then I suggest you lads go on foot. Ben, get the engine turned around and we'll see you there.'

We did as we were told. The old codger couldn't hope to keep up with our march. But he tried, bless him. You can't keep that kind down, thank God. His funny tweed cape strung out in the air behind him as he broke into a trot. And he did have help picking up a bit of speed. His slavering, shivering, salivating dog was desperate to beat everyone round the corner. He was pulling so hard he nearly dragged his owner off his feet

– while all but strangling himself in the process. It was clear this was the most excitement he'd had in years. He didn't want to miss a thing.

Two hundred yards turned into at least three hundred by the time we saw the house up ahead. The old geezer had certainly been right about the smoke. It was billowing up into the sky like billy-o, mushrooming above the roof from somewhere at the back of the property. But I think we all knew, even from a distance, that the old guy had made a second mistake.

'Off you go, lads,' yelled Joe, just as Ben swept past us in the water tender and sliced into the soft grass verge.

The house was the left-hand half of a traditional semi. The gate at the side was open, so we piled through it and were soon in the rear garden looking up. That's when things calmed down. This house didn't actually have a chimney either – again, a bit of an oversight for a chimney fire. But it did have a boiler vent sticking out through the roof at the rear elevation. That was where the smoke was coming from – and as we got to the back of the house we confirmed what we'd already suspected. This was probably steam, not smoke.

'That's water vapour. It's only the boiler,' said Charlie decisively. I knew he was probably right. You can tell by the way steam moves. Plus of course it dissipates, while smoke hangs around.

'There's an awful lot of it,' said our elderly neighbour.

'It's cold out here today, that's why it's not dissipating as quickly as normal. It's steam. I tell you, there's nothing going on.'

'Worth checking out all the same. Let's see if we can get in there,' Joe said firmly. This was looking like a classic 'false alarm, good intent' shout. But the last thing we wanted to do was to turn up somewhere, miss something, drive away and leave a worse problem for someone else to tackle later.

Joe, Pete and I headed to the front door to bang on it and confirm that there was no one home. Once we'd done that, we'd decide if we needed to push our way in. Credit cards really did open plenty of locks back then, and we had other tools that could open up gaps in doors then spring them. Worst-case scenario, if we needed to get into a house to do our job, we'd smash the glass in a door and get access to the handle. Or we'd do the full hero routine and smash the door down altogether. Fortunately, we hadn't quite got that far on this occasion. Because the door opened just as we were turning away from it to consider our next move.

A small, squat woman with tight, dark curly hair stood there, mouth wide open. 'Oi! What are you lot doing in my garden?' she said when she collected her thoughts.

'We've had a fire reported in your house and we're here to investigate,' said Joe, hiding his surprise well.

The woman managed to look horrified, confused and mildly disbelieving all at once. 'A fire? In my house? I don't think so. I've just got in from the shops two minutes ago and made a pot of tea for my two girls. They're doing their homework in the back room. Everything is fine.'

'Have you been upstairs since you got in?'

'The girls went up to their bedrooms and the bathroom I think. There's nothing wrong. I swear there isn't.'

Joe smiled, firm but fair. 'Well, there seems to be a lot of steam coming from your boiler.'

'It always does that. It drives me mad. You should see what the place looks like when I turn the tumble drier on.'

'All the same, I'd like to send in one of my men to give the property the once-over. He can confirm that everything is safe and sound.'

The woman looked slightly doubtful. She glanced at the fire engine and the rest of us and then made her decision. If this was some sort of scam or wind-up then it was a pretty complex one. There had to be easier ways to burgle someone than to get five guys together and turn up at your door in full fire kit on a gleaming red fire engine. So she stood aside. 'Of course. Come right in, sorry about the mess,' she said, slightly embarrassed as Pete stepped up and disappeared through the front door.

Out in the street our wizard lookalike was beside himself with embarrassment. 'They must have returned while I was calling you from the phone box. I never thought to bash on the door again and check it was still empty. You must think me a terrible fool. But it still doesn't look as if anyone is home, does it? The whole street seemed deserted. I do hope I've not done something silly.' His voice was breaking a bit now, as we waited for Pete to come out and give us the all-clear. 'Are you sure it's not a fire?' he asked plaintively, as the minutes passed and the steam carried on rising from the vent. 'It looks like a fire, right enough.'

'Central heating systems often do when the weather is on the cold side,' said Joe kindly. 'I really don't think there's any danger of a fire.'

At which point Pete came pounding out of the front door and down the front path.

'You're never going to believe it, boss – it's a fire! A big one!' he said. And suddenly all hell broke loose.

# 24

# The Next Surprise

∞

Pete was shouting loudly now. 'It really is a fire. Looks like there's a whole load of junk in the attic – boxes of Christmas decorations, clothes, bedding, other stuff. It's all piled up against the boiler. It's caught and it's spreading. The boiler must have malfunctioned or something. That's why it's been chucking out so much steam.'

Joe moved fast. He ran to the water tender, got on the radio and sent a 'Make pumps two' call to Control to get another engine on its way, plus a turntable ladder to help with access and ripping roof tiles off if required.

The rest of us did what we were trained to do. We made sure the owner and her daughters got out of the house and moved safely away. Then two of us pulled on our breathing apparatus sets, handed over our tallies and dragged the hose-reel into the house to fight the fire. It turned out we'd arrived in the nick of time. The downstairs and the first floor were smoke and damage free. But the attic was in bad shape – and it was easy to see why. It was a big space, and it was packed with the kind of junk that people put in their attics. Precisely the kind of lovely, tinder-dry, toasty hot and highly flammable junk that fires love.

The fire certainly loved this stuff. The attic was full of dense smoke. Visibility was shocking, so it was hard to determine the exact scale of the fire. But it was clear it was bigger than we'd expected – and it was getting bigger and hotter at a rate of knots.

'Over this side,' I shouted to Pete, though I doubted he could hear me through our masks, and the sound of the fire.

We were starting to get more water where we needed it when I finally managed to hear something from Pete. 'Bloody hell, my foot!' he cried out. I didn't need to look across to know what had happened. Fighting fires in attics brings a range of extra hazards. When the room hasn't been floored out, as this one hadn't, you've got to balance on the wooden joists. One slip and your big size-twelve fireman's boot plunges into the sea of fibreglass everyone uses as insulation and through to the bedroom ceiling below.

'Nearly lost it then,' Pete muttered, pulling his foot up and regaining his balance.

We carried on with our work, but the writing was effectively on that attic wall by then. This was no longer an inside job. It was too big to be tackled from within the confines of a packed, hazard-filled room. If we were to save the house, we'd have to fight it from outside as well.

In the street, Joe and John were in full command and control mode as the other appliances turned up and the guys quickly got the turntable ladder up and ready. As soon as it was in place, Martin was on the end of it, prising big concrete tiles off the roof to make an opening. When that was done we could not only ventilate the smoke but also aim a hose in from above.

'Mum! Look what they're doing to our roof! Mum, they're going to knock the house down!' one of the daughters was saying as this process began.

'Don't be stupid,' she snapped back. 'They're just— they're just—' She stopped and gazed across at Joe. 'You're not knocking the house down, are you?'

'Not if we can help it,' he said, not offering quite as much reassurance as the woman had hoped for.

We got the hose-reel up to the head of the TL so Martin could aim it through the hole he had opened up. If the family had been lucky at this point, the water would have got to every part of the fire and the job would have been all but over. The family weren't lucky.

'The fire's been going a lot longer than it looks. There's significant damage to the roof joists,' Martin reported down as he did his work. 'It's got to be structurally unsafe.'

There was a pause for more information and then a decision from Joe. 'Strip the roof completely,' he said. And so, one by one, the tiles on that side were taken off and stacked on the ladder. When the overload warning light came on, the TL was brought down, the tiles were unloaded, and then the process began again.

'This simply cannot be happening to me. This has to be a dream, or a nightmare. I was about to peel some spuds. It was homework time. We were sitting down, having a nice cup of tea. Ten minutes later you're taking my roof off. My husband will go spare. He's going to come home from work to see we don't have a roof any more. And I didn't even know the house was on fire!' the woman kept saying.

She wasn't the only one rambling.

'I thought your house was on fire, then I was told it wasn't, and now it turns out that it was. My head is starting to hurt. I don't know if I'm coming or going any more,' our dog walker pitched in.

And there was still one more surprise to come.

# 25

# The Bombshell

∞

The police and ambulance had joined us and a loose cordon had been set up to keep the onlookers at a safe distance. Nonetheless a car came right up to it and the driver got out to take a long, slow look at what was going on. He was a round, bearded guy who moved slowly and methodically. He had an ex-military air about him.

'That's my house,' he said, pointing to the other half of the semi-detached home. He didn't ask any questions or say anything else for a while. He didn't seem remotely bothered by the drama. Then he got back in his car and drove it onto his drive. He parked, climbed out and locked the door slowly. Turning, he gave a nod to some of the people in the small crowd of onlookers that had gathered on the far side of the street.

One of the police went up to tell him to keep away from his house while the operation continued. He nodded and shrugged then ambled slowly across to us. 'A fire,' he said, helpfully, when he arrived.

'The attic's on fire. Bit of a problem with their boiler and a load of paper and other junk that was stacked up against it. We've got it under control. You live next door?' asked Joe.

'I certainly do.'

'Anyone at home now?'

'Not unless there's burglars and I'm being robbed.'

'Then perhaps you can wait around here for a while and steer clear of your property. Just until we get everything fully under control.'

The man shrugged. Apparently quite happy to comply, he stepped back and nodded his head as if he didn't have a care in the world. He shared a few words with our dog walker and some of the other neighbours who had come out to watch. Then he stepped forward again. 'The fire's not spreading, then?' he asked, almost as an afterthought.

'Not if we can help it,' said Joe.

'That's good news,' the neighbour said in a soft, slow voice. He was nodding his head to himself again. 'Because I've got four hundred rounds of ammunition in my half of the attic next door. We wouldn't really want those involved in your fire now, would we?' he said, once more as if it were an afterthought.

While the man himself seemed completely untroubled, the rest of us froze at his words. Even the old guy's dog seemed to grasp the significance. I swear his helicopter tail stopped wagging for a moment and his shiny eyes looked right at the ammo-filled attic in question.

'Ammunition, you say?' Joe asked slowly.

'That's right.'

'Four hundred rounds of it?'

'Aye. Guns too. It's all in my attic.'

There was the shortest of pauses before Joe spoke again. 'Are the attics connected? Can you walk through? Or is there a dividing wall?'

'There's a dividing wall. Of sorts,' he said vaguely.

'Of sorts?' spluttered Joe. This did not sound good.

John and Joe quickly got their heads together and came

up with a plan. Everything was speeding up again, the way it always did when events took you unawares.

Pete and I were sent back into the first house to give the party wall an even more thorough dousing with water. Any sign of a breach and we were to report it straight away.

'This could be fun,' Pete said on the upstairs landing as we got ready to climb up into the attic.

Fun probably wasn't the right word. Is it fun to stand on top of a ladder and poke your head into a room that could be tooled up like a domestic version of Arnold Schwarzenegger?

But at least Pete and I were on the safer side of the house. The unlucky one was the poor sod who was charged with poking his head into the gun-toting neighbour's attic.

'Nicholas, I think this is a job for you,' Joe said when he assigned our roles.

I can't repeat what Nicholas said in reply.

I do remember what he said after he'd stepped up to the task, however. 'There's a lot of smoke in there,' he reported, having shone his torch into all corners of the neighbouring attic. That was not good. If smoke could make its way from one attic to the next, then perhaps the fire could.

Funny how the presence of ammunition and guns encourages you to put fires out even faster than normal. Pete and I got the rest of that first attic soaked and sorted in record time – backed up by Martin's efforts from outside. Then, with the smoke clearing from the skylight Martin had created, we gave the party wall a proper check from that side. It was hot. It had taken a beating. But it looked solid.

The work went on for some time, but after a certain point we knew we had won – and not a single shot had been fired. 'We'll help fix some of the mess for you, love,' Joe had said to the mum a while ago – just after she gave in to the shock of it all and started to cry. We're never obligated to do total clear-up jobs after a fire, but we always clear out the burnt debris and try to make the property weather-proof once again before we leave. The mum from the first house had been nice as pie, so we did our best for her. A heck of a lot of water had flooded in through the top of her house. So there was a heck of a lot of water damage throughout. Then there was the hole in her roof. We got a load of plastic sixteen-by-sixteen salvage sheets to cover up the worst of it.

Her laconic, gun-loving neighbour was a different matter. He'd not done anything to annoy or irritate us. But he'd not covered himself in glory. He'd not offered to put the kettle on for us either, even though his kitchen was untouched. So we simply passed him on to the coppers for a chat about how he stored his kit in the future and just what he had there in the first place.

The last person we saw before leaving was our one man and his dog. His face was worried, the way it had been the whole time. His dog was still off-the-scale happy with life, the universe and everything. 'It all seems to have gone from one thing to the other. I was wrong about there being a fire, but I was right about it as well. And I did do the right thing in calling you, didn't I?' he asked as we prepared to leave.

'You certainly did, sir,' said Joe, while the mad greyhound set to work licking through the knee-pads on his overalls.

I was still grinning as we piled into the engine and headed back to base. It was almost exactly five o'clock. We'd probably have a cup of tea and a laugh about the day, then we'd head off – and I'd start packing for my holiday.

It had been another brilliant day. A chimney fire in a house without a chimney, an empty house that turned out to anything but – and an attic full of ammo. Seven years as a fireman and the job could still surprise me every day. Best job in the world.

For competitions, author interviews,
pre-publication extracts, news and events,
sign up to the monthly

**Orion Books Newsletter**

at

# www.orionbooks.co.uk

Prefer your updates daily?
Follow us @orionbooks